ADVANTAGE

HARNESSING CUMULATIVE ADVANTAGE IN THE WINNER-TAKES-ALL PUBLISHING MARKET

JOE SOLARI

Claymore Ulfberht & Xiphos LLC

"There are only two mistakes one can make along the road to truth; not going all the way, and not starting."

Buddha

Copyright © 2020 by Joe Solari

All rights reserved.

No part of this book may be reproduced in any form or by any electronic or mechanical means, including information storage and retrieval systems, without written permission from the author, except for the use of brief quotations in a book review.

Take Your Publishing Business to the Next Level

Learn how to build a better publishing business

ARE YOU PART OF THE HERD OR LEADING YOUR PACK?

 "A person who won't read has no advantage over one who can't read."

— *MARK TWAIN*

Does this book hold the secrets to you dominating the Amazon bookstore?

The next few moments will determine if you'll part with your money to purchase this book. Will what I've written fulfill your desire to sell more books? You want to succeed as an author so bad, it has driven you to explore the dark arts of marketing and advertising.

You might have heard about this book from another author, or found it through a suggestion from an online bookstore. Now you browse the inside to confirm the recommendation.

If you buy this book, my job isn't done until I deliver on its promise. Yes, I've achieved a sale, but your trust has yet to be earned. So, what is that promise?

I will show you how to separate yourself from the pack of those seeking the next hack, or marketing gimmick. I'll show you the way to become the leader of your own pack of fans desperate for your next book.

If you're like most authors, you're confounded how some climb the bestseller ranks, getting more popular with each launch, while you seem to be stuck or always one step behind the crowd. This book illuminates the path to you commanding that kind of advantage in the marketplace. While the quality of your books is the prime determinate of success, I can promise that what you'll learn in *Advantage* is the easiest way to build your audience.

If your marketing and advertising isn't working as it used to, the failure isn't your poor application. Instead, it is the product of thousands of other authors applying the same methods and creating herd immunity in the reader community. Our collective onslaught makes readers tired of hard-sells and calls to action. Your efforts look and smell like all the other digital marketing flooding social media.

If the adage that only six degrees of separation exist between you and any other person on the planet, then why is it so hard to find new readers?

Maybe it's not finding them, but getting them to *act*.

To complicate matters, research suggests that social media hinder your ability to get a reader to buy and read your book. What if I were to show you that social media platforms that connect more people faster, harm rather than help your cause?

The reason most promotions on social media don't go viral is that none of the critical groundwork exists. For your marketing to be contagious, it needs to be more than persuasive. You must create the conditions for a complex contagion to spread. Consumers are exposed to millions of these contagions daily, and they have developed a strong resistance to digital marketing.

Your ideas don't spread like a virus. Instead, it is closer to a wildfire. Without the right conditions, an ignition source can start a fire, but it won't create a firestorm. Conversely, the longer the conditions build, the better the results once ignition occurs. Work done this season that doesn't result in a fire contributes to better results in future seasons.

To make matters worse, as a later entrant into publishing, it feels like others are so far ahead you'll never catch up. In the end, all the spoils will end up going to a select few because of uncaring market amplified by opaque technology never giving you a fair chance.

> **Imagine yourself harnessing the same dominant force that drives 64% of the profits into the hands of 2.5% of published authors.**

The publishing market is driven by a market force that leverages past success in future rounds. If you sell genre fiction or are attempting to build a following on YouTube or Instagram, you face this formidable economic influence. The spoils go to a few who become famous.

This popularity – sometimes called the superstar effect, or cumulative advantage – is the sorting system in arts, sports, and entertainment. Cumulative advantage is the hurricane that can crush your boat or provide an endless supply of wind for your sails.

HOW DO YOU CAPTURE ITS POWER?

I work with authors who make six-figure profits. As their business strategist, I've observed how they build cumulative advantage to be regularly propelled into the of top 100 bestselling authors in the entire Kindle bookstore.

While researching this book, I uncovered the underlying principles of successfully accumulating advantage in the publishing market. It's not how you use a particular social media platform or where you advertise.

I want to be clear: this isn't a marketing book that provides marketing or advertising tactics, although once you understand the principles, I'll show you how a virtuous marketing cycle becomes your cumulative advantage engine.

I have determined that not only can cumulative advantage be systematized, but a unique flavor is possible for every author. Best of all, you already possess the key to unlocking its power. You can take control of the monolithic market force of cumulative advantage and bend it to your will.

It will take unlearning and relearning, but if you are prepared to join me on the journey to where this key is hidden, you will be surprised at how well suited you are to wielding it for the benefit of yourself and your readers.

If you read this entire book, I will introduce you to the concepts of cognitive bias, networks, and crowd behavior. What you learn on these topics will become the foundation for a lasting brand. This book shows you how to construct a unique process to connect with and engage an audience. The system will pass the test of time; even as others adopt learning from this book, your work won't be diluted, because of the connection between your brand and what your readers desire.

There have been dozens of books written about what makes an idea powerful or the importance of triggering a tipping point for an information cascade. The problem with those books is they never shed light on how to cause that tipping point.

In this book I'll show you how to trigger cumulative advantage. You will learn how to get existing readers to trust you and take responsibility to find you new readers. You will learn to build a network – not one built on social media (although you may use it as a tool), but one built on meeting human needs. The system will be reliable and resistant to damage. Messages sent through the network will be trusted and get to the right person. You will create a valuable asset for your business that will adapt to changes in technology and serve you for your entire career. Best of all, this work will fuel the flywheel of cumulative advantage. As time passes, sales will come faster and easier.

In publishing, the disconnect is between what you want versus what the reader wants. Satisfying a reader may seem obvious now that you read it here, but when you look at most author advertising and marketing, it is focused on the transaction.

Readers don't want to buy books. They want satisfying entertainment through reading. They will pay money to you if you can deliver. Therefore, your marketing needs to put the desired activity foremost, not the act of buying. Associating your book and brand with the desired result closes the loop. The transaction becomes a small step for the reader to get what they want.

This book offers the *why* and *how* of building cumulative advantage.

I can show you how a series of *slight changes* in how you act and think about book marketing will build into a substantial organic following.

Now is the time to act. You have to choose to:

- do nothing, falling further and further behind,
- follow the crowd and implement this week's marketing tip until it becomes market noise,
- or join me on a journey deep into the mind of your reader where your cumulative advantage hides.

I can guide you, just as I've guided other authors on this journey to discover their source of cumulative advantage. The journey starts at the lofty heights of the marketplace, where cumulative advantage rules the roost. Together, we will descend deep into the inner workings of this market force to see how a reader's behavior and feelings drive it. Once you possess this knowledge, you can accumulate a growing organic following that sees you as the leader of their pack, and the pack as part of their own identity.

Are you ready to begin this journey?

CONTENTS

ARE YOU PART OF THE HERD OR LEADING YOUR PACK?	1
How do you capture its power?	3
INTRODUCTION	11
One more thing: Why listen to me?	14
THE MACROSCOPIC LAYER	15
1. HOW BIG IS THE PUBLISHING INDUSTRY?	16
Scope and Scale	17
Can I help you find what you're looking for?	19
The Harsh Reality	21
2. A CLASH OF TITANS	24
It's Not the Cliff, It's Gravity that Kills You	25
The Binge Economy	26
Establishing a Rank Plateau	32
3. WINNER TAKES ALL: UNDERSTANDING CUMULATIVE ADVANTAGE	34
Papa Pareto, the Father of Power Laws	38
What is a Power Law?	39
Where Does a Bestseller's Power Come From?	42
How Does Cumulative Advantage Form?	44
Size and Scale	46
Is it talent?	47
Will this system guarantee you will become a bestseller?	51
4. IS THERE A FORMULA FOR RECOGNITION AND POPULARITY?	54
What will it take to make your brand or books as iconic as Albert Einstein?	59
5. SAY MY NAME: HOW TRENDS DEVELOP AND WHY IT'S IMPORTANT TO YOU	61
A Niece Named Emma	63
Popular Culture	67

Invisible Forces	69
Is fanaticism the way to convert a society?	71

THE MESOSCOPIC LAYER — 73

6. YOUR BRAND — 74
- Where does your brand come from? — 75
- A Brand Promise Kept — 76
- Welcome to your brand fantasy — 78
- Defining your tribe — 79

7. YOUR COMMUNITY — 81
- Your Social Brain — 81
- Why do you need a Community? — 82
- Don't Mistake Social Media for Community or Platform. — 82
- Stop Gumming Up the Works — 85
- The Other Villainous Force: Inertia — 86
- The Meso-Neuro Feedback Loop and How to Create Cumulative Advantage. — 94

THE MICROSCOPIC LAYER — 97

8. IT'S ALL IN YOUR HEAD — 98
- Here lies the power of a storyteller. — 109

9. YOUR SECRET WEAPON — 111
- Blurring the Lines — 114

UP FROM THE DEPTHS — 117

10. USING THE KEY — 118
- Dopamine = Desire — 119
- Pattern Matching — 119
- How Do You Use Pattern Matching? — 121
- Priming and Fluency — 122

UNLOCKING CUMULATIVE ADVANTAGE — 127

11. ZIG WHEN OTHERS ZAG? — 128
- It's Pay to Play — 129
- The Battle Between Apple, Google, and Facebook — 130
- A Rising Tide aka Regressing to the Mean — 131
- Boy, Are You Stacked — 132
- Reduced Gross Margin and Impact on Cash Flow — 133
- Is There Any Correlation Between Ad Spend and Sales? — 133

12. A VICIOUS OR VIRTUOUS MARKETING CYCLE — 136
- The Vicious Marketing Cycle — 136
- The Virtuous Marketing Cycle — 138

13. The Process	141
14. EMBEDDING CUMULATIVE ADVANTAGE IN YOUR CONTENT	143
Do You Satisfy Your Reader?	143
Story Arc, Tropes, and Metonyms	144
Character Archetypes and Para-Social Relationships	146
Lore and Canon	149
15. HOW TO CREATE A COMMUNITY THAT BECOMES A FEEDBACK LOOP FOR CUMULATIVE ADVANTAGE	151
What Should My Community Look Like?	152
Using a Common Para-Social Connection as the Network Broker for Your Community.	153
Fulfilling a Social Need	153
Building the Community	154
The Human Givens Within the Community	157
Become a Social Network Designer	158
Homophily and Heterogeneity	161
Understanding Not Applying Pressure	164
Signaling and Triggering Behavior	165
What Roles Does Your Group Require?	166
Building Sub-Networks	168
Identify the Movers and Shakers	169
Group Identity	170
Self-directed Behavior	170
Behaviors and Activities	170
Ways to Define Your Tribe	176
16. WHAT IS YOUR BRAND PROMISE, AND DO YOU DELIVER?	177
Brand Promise	178
Brand Fantasy	178
A Brand Bible	179
17. MAKING IT HAPPEN: BUILDING YOUR CUMULATIVE ADVANTAGE ENGINE	180
The Virtuous Marketing Cycle	181
The Connective Tissue - Human Givens	182
18. START	183
Compelling Fiction	183
Identifying Your Market	184
A Release Strategy	184

What Should You Spend Your Money On?	185
Product Production and Quality	185
Finding Your Audience	185
Email	186
19. LAUNCH	188
Preorders	189
Advertising	189
Celebrations and Contests	189
Budget	191
20. ACCUMULATE	192
Email	193
Community	193
21. INDOCTRINATE	194
Organic Indoctrination	195
Segment	195
Using Character and Story World to Segment	196
Working Your Back Catalog	196
Begin With the End in Mind	197
22. Re(enter)tain	198
23. What About Non-Fiction?	200
Afterword	203
Acknowledgments	207
About the Author	209
Also by Joe Solari	211
Notes	213
Bibliography	219

INTRODUCTION

> "If my answers frighten you then cease asking scary questions."
> Jules, Pulp Fiction

Do you find yourself posting questions to your favorite author group about fixing some recent snafu in your Facebook ads, or spending hours trying to write the perfect sales page copy to get a higher conversion rate? No wonder you're losing your love of writing.

While independent publishing has made it possible for authors to get their books to market, it has also made it so they are responsible for more tasks beyond writing. If you're like most authors, you feel that it's an eighty-twenty split of duties, with the eighty percent being all of the publishing activities required to get your books to sell. It's enough to make you give up.

How often do you try some tactic that the author community is raving about and it falls flat for you? Are you wondering what the next steps are on this journey? Do you just give up? Should you buy one more course?

I have committed to guiding you through a journey of discovery—a trip from ordinary to exceptional results. From obscurity to achieving category and store bestseller lists. To complete this journey, you need to learn about what drives the publishing market, and why a small fraction of authors get most of the profits.

Cumulative advantage is the name given to the force that drives winner-take-most markets. It has been in play for centuries in publishing, and will continue to drive industry results regardless of how you go to market.

Now, you may feel it is unfair that only a few get the spoils, but if you are going to get hung up on fairness and equality, then cumulative advantage already has you beat.

Others discovered the existence of cumulative advantage in the publishing market. I'll be citing research that shows its existence and power go back hundreds of years. You'll also see proof of its massive impact in today's digital book market.

Some studies suggest[1] that in digital markets, cumulative advantage is amplified, concentrating popularity and wealth even further. It was in working with clients already reaching the top of bestseller lists and earning hundreds of thousands of dollars in profit that I could understand how cumulative advantage can be used to your benefit.

As I learned how cumulative advantage worked, it became clear that this relentless force was the chief ingredient of success. Rather than fight it, I wanted to discover how to use its momentum to propel an author's popularity. How can this be done with such a fickle and unfair foe?

Here is where I will start with the unlearning process. Don't get hung up on fairness or equality. Cumulative advantage is blind to these ideas. No committee or company controls it; it is driven by the consensus of buyers in the market. It is unique in that there is a positive feedback loop; over time, the collective decisions of the group influence the future choices of individuals.

Rather than whine about the unfairness cumulative advantage exhibits, deny its existence, or call for its abolition, we will embrace its power and become its master. Best of all is that my research shows that authors can control accumulation like no other creator.

Here is a question for you. Do you believe that we should reward a person for their merit?

So does cumulative advantage.

Cumulative advantage exists in markets where the individual choice of buyers is to go with what is most popular or performs the best. It is dominant in the arts, entertainment, sports, and investment. We want the best for ourselves, and so do others, so we come to a collective conclusion of what is 'best'. The result is the market settles on a few suppliers rather than equally matching supply to the demand of the market.

I will be your mentor and guide on a journey to where your secret power to manipulate cumulative advantage hides. This journey will take you through three layers. The first is the macroscopic layer, where we will explore and break down how the publishing market works and how popularity, recognition and social convention drive the market. The next stop is the mesoscopic layer, where we will unpack how brand and social networks work. It will shock you to learn that a lot of what you do for marketing is killing your chances to take control of cumulative advantage. Here you will see research on how to build a system that supports building cumulative advantage and gets readers to connect with your brand. The last layer is the microscopic layer; I sometimes call it the neuroscopic layer. It is where you will discover how to influence behavior through the way your stories are processed inside the brain of a reader. It is here that you'll find that the unconscious mind, not rational thought, drives the buying decision.

With knowledge from all three layers in hand, you'll possess the key to unlocking cumulative advantage.

I hate books that tell you why but never tell you how. As I researched this book, I read countless scientific papers loaded with formulas and statistics. It has become clear to me that there is very little information on the "how-to" of cumulative advantage. Researchers can identify it, quantify it, but none provide methods to generate or leverage the market force. Therefore, in the last section, you'll see my process for making it happen. I'll share how the virtuous marketing cycle differs from the commonly used vicious marketing cycle, and how you can build your virtuous marketing system.

While this may seem like this is going to be a lot of work, it isn't. Much of the process is going to be unlearning and relearning, shifting your understanding of the market, and getting you to see the Matrix, so like Neo, you can manipulate the binding force of the market to do your bidding.

ONE MORE THING: WHY LISTEN TO ME?

There is no end to the number of people telling you how to succeed. So why should you see me as a credible mentor?

I've had decades of experience as a small business owner. I've bought and sold businesses and raised millions of dollars. After selling my last company, I got involved in the author community to help authors build better businesses.

Since 2016 I've helped authors at every level to be better at the business of writing, and that includes those who are earning six and seven figures. I've worked with them mainly on their behind-the-scenes: operations, cash-flow, taxes… you know, the fun stuff. I also help my clients with the broader goal of growing their business. It is from this work that I've compiled the research in this book. It was working with these authors that I've seen the forces I describe in action, and have used the practices I'll share to cut advertising costs, build brand loyalty, and establish direct sales with readers.

Now, you may say, *"Of course it's easy to build cumulative advantage when you already have it."* You would be right, it's way easier. But every one of my clients started out the same way: unpublished, with no audience. They found success without this roadmap.

With an understanding of how this market force is created, I was able to go back and validate my discoveries through interviews with my clients, and help them see why what they did worked. You now get the benefit of this learning to use cumulative advantage to drive your publishing business.

Enough about my clients and me, let's get you started on accumulating *your* advantage.

THE MACROSCOPIC LAYER

Where cumulative advantage influences the market at large.

1
HOW BIG IS THE PUBLISHING INDUSTRY?

> "The truth is rarely pure and never simple."
>
> — OSCAR WILDE, THE IMPORTANCE OF BEING EARNEST

Before we dive into the inner workings of cumulative advantage, we will need to establish common ground on what is happening at the macroscopic layer of publishing. I will also share with you my conclusions about the global publishing marketplace, and how I think your talent, skill, and luck influence performance.

The macroscopic layer is where colossal forces are in conflict. Rank gravity pulls all published works towards the black hole of obscurity, while cumulative advantage drives a select few up into the stratosphere of the bestseller list. The consequence of these forces is shocking when you recognize that they are picking the winners and losers in a multibillion-dollar market.

SCOPE AND SCALE

When thinking of the marketplace for your stories, it is far bigger than what you see in the Amazon bookstore, but keep in mind I will reference the Kindle Marketplace as a real-time model of the entire publishing market.

The book publishing market has gross sales somewhere between fifty and one hundred billion dollars a year. I can't give you a specific number because there isn't a single source that does a suitable job to assess the market.

If you are prepared to think of yourself as a content creator and are open to other media such as audiobooks, video games, movies, and television, then the market gets significantly bigger. Include experiences like theme parks and merchandising, and we are now looking at a trillion-dollar global market.

I am prepared to argue that while I focus on book marketing, the principles in this book apply to the entire content consumption/experience marketplace. As the entertainment market grows, the demand for story in other media will increase. The only thing that separates your dreams of building a media empire from reality is the work to make it happen. I know more than one author who is transitioning their business from just books to a media experience empire.

Why I like to focus on the Amazon Kindle Market is because it is a nearly real-time model of book retailing, and we can analyze it. Think of Amazon's ranking of books as a stock market ticker of book and author popularity.

Here are some of its features the make it interesting:

1. **The data set:** In October 2019, Amazon accounted for fifty-two percent of all books sold in the United States. From a statistics viewpoint, that means that data is statistically significant and provides a nearly perfect picture of the marketplace. In fact, most of the book sales pass through the platform.
2. **Measurement:** The bookstore on Amazon is interesting

because it ranks all books, and aligns the hierarchy by sales performance. We can use this ranking system to evaluate performance and map out what the market looks like now, or how it has changed over time.
3. **Update rate:** Outside of a glitch from time to time, the ranking system appears to be reliable and updated hourly. This living rank system allows us to see changes in small time segments.
4. **Breadth of Offering:** This marketplace is diverse. It may not appear so at first glance because of cumulative advantage, but there are over four million titles on Amazon in either ebook, mass-market print, or print on demand.

In October 2004, Chris Anderson published his article in Wired called *"The Long Tail"*.[1] The concept of the long tail is that by having a wide range of niche products available for customers to access, you create a competitive advantage. In fact, this was part of Jeff Bezos' thesis when selecting books as the first products on Amazon.

When Amazon first launched, the typical brick and mortar bookstores carried 175,000 SKUs while there were over 3,000,000 books in print. The average Barnes and Noble stocked about five percent of published books, and they skewed their inventory toward the most popular titles. Amazon brought product diversity to the market by efficiently selling niche products and exploiting the long tail.

Brynjolfsson, Hu, and Smith published research in 2010 that suggests that the long tail phenomena created a customer surplus of three to five billion dollars of sales in 2008 that would not have existed under the traditional brick and mortar sales strategy.

"We find that the Long Tail has grown longer over time, with niche books accounting for a larger share of total sales. Our analyses suggest that by 2008, niche books account for 36.7% of Amazon's sales, and the consumer surplus generated by niche books has increased at least fivefold from 2000 to 2008."[2]

Amazon presents the most diverse book title offering in history. Therefore, it can be deduced that the ranking system is an indicator of the hour by hour popularity of all available books. Furthermore, there is a constant flow of new products being uploaded, making it the most up to date market. Estimates are that over 88,000 titles release per month[3]. Amazon has become the de facto marketplace.

The bestseller list is the head of a very long tail. To reach a rank in the top ten, you must sell 800 to 1000 books in a day. There is a range because all ranking is relative and at the highest ranks, it depends what books have released.

It takes approximately a sale a day for a book to hold a position of 100,000 (this has been sliding down because of the number of books published). Selling a book a day works out to somewhere around two thousand dollars a year in royalties. By looking at rank, we know that 97.5% of books sell less than one book a day. On any day, 2.5% of the published books capture 64% of the revenue. It could be higher, but Brynjolfsson's research suggests that Amazon derives 36% of its profit from the long tail.

CAN I HELP YOU FIND WHAT YOU'RE LOOKING FOR?

Search engine technology makes catalog searches of products by title and keywords easier, and allows buyers to find products that meet their interests. Without a method of quickly connecting supply and demand, there would be little value provided by having so many products to choose from.

A second and equally powerful algorithm propels sales of niche products on Amazon. Anderson mentioned its use in his *Long Tail* article, where he shared how Amazon could turn a nearly out-of-print book like *Into the Void* into a bestseller because of the popularity of *Into Thin Air*. The association of the two mountain-climbing books shows the power of identifying purchasing associations, then suggesting them to similar readers. To this day, the *also bought* suggestions on a sales page and in marketing emails are critical to driving sales for Amazon.

Search and suggestion play to one of our natural limits, the size of anyone's agenda. This means it is beyond your capacity to review all the possible options.

Humans become overwhelmed with too much choice. Searching gives you a false sense of satisfying your agenda. Unconsciously, you know that you have limited capacity to search through all options. You trust that search and suggestion will deliver a suitable solution. Even though you're shown only a small subset of choices, you feel satisfied that you've done your best to review options.

In reality, Amazon and authors are working to give you more of what they think you want, thereby reducing choice. Amazon will continue to refine search to connect customers to products. As machine learning improves, so will the results that product searches deliver to the searcher.

The Amazon algorithm gets a lot of the blame for what happens to book demand. While it amplifies cumulative advantage, it isn't hiding books or dropping them off cliffs. Read a post on book marketing or listen to the experts, and you'd think Amazon's ranking system is the only thing that matters for selling a book. While it is a powerful influence on visibility, the recommendation algorithms won't protect you from rank gravity. On the contrary, they give you a false sense of interest.

No amount of worshiping to the machine god will stop the inevitable pull toward an ever-increasing rank number (remember, a lower rank number is better) and your book's descent into Amazon's virtual bargain basement.

One explanation is that Amazon loves new products and they present them over older existing products. There is truth to this, as without some preference to new products all we would see in the same old best sellers. Therefore, new products get a short-term boost to help them find an audience and create product diversity in the store. This can lead to the misconception that after this preferential treatment your book drops out of new product lists and loses visibility. This is commonly referred to as dropping off the cliff. I have evidence that, as powerful as Amazon's marketing is, there is a natural market force, like gravity, always pulling books toward a larger rank number. What you experience as the 30,60, or 90-day cliff is the short-term rank boost of your existing audience consuming your book.

Without consistent daily sales, your book will begin its rank decay, falling from whatever altitude it reached to a rank plateau.

THE HARSH REALITY

To make matters worse, the marketplace for books isn't a level playing field. First off, the whole market is tilted toward the dominant sales platform of Amazon. Furthermore, unlike a game of Monopoly where everyone starts with the same money at the same spot and at the same time, you are joining a game already in play. As a new entrant, this is discouraging, but that discouragement comes from comparison and a desire for fairness.

Comparison is the thief of joy. The mood it creates isn't one that will motivate you. Fairness is an ideal and rarely found in the market. Instead, go into this with eyes wide open, and an acceptance that you are on *your* path, and need to work *your* way up. Top tennis players understand that while they may not be number one now, the only way to the top is to play the game.

Who is the holder of the most Grand Slam titles? At the time of this writing, that would be Margaret Court, who holds sixty-four titles. Serena Williams, who is still active and is closing in on Margaret's record, may one day surpass her. While the ranking system in professional tennis provides the hierarchy of tennis talent, it is a snapshot in time. Even in the number one spot, there is variation in what it takes to hold the spot, and who holds that spot.

It takes on average, 4.5 years for a tennis player to reach the top 100 after going professional[4]. That means it takes nearly five years to find out if you are one of thousands of excellent players, or one of one hundred elite players guaranteed to make money. As a player works up the ranks, she gains cumulative advantage over others. Just like in the author marketplace, the focus is on the levels that are hardest to attain and the most visible, held by a few.

When looking at the total population of ranked tennis players, only a fraction of a percentage point makes it to the top ranks. Those top-ranked players get invited to tournaments with the most substantial prizes and get contracts for endorsements.

Rather than focusing on comparison and fairness as you enter the marketplace, look at talent, skill, and luck. These three factors have far more to do with your success than fairness does.

Back to our example of a tennis player, each player has a natural talent for playing the game. Talent is the primary driver of success, but there is more to success; it is part skill and part luck. Skill is learned and improves with practice. It comes from playing the game. The tougher the opponents you play, the more experience you gain. Skill can be so powerful that it offsets lost performance from age and injuries.

The last factor is luck. Luck is a funny thing. We take credit for what good luck gives us, and rationalize lack of skill or talent as poor luck. One important takeaway is to work on being objective about the part luck plays in your success. Skill, talent, and planning will tilt probability in your favor, but sometimes you roll the dice and land on your opponent's fully developed boardwalk.

This book and the work you do after you read it will build your cumulative advantage creation skill. Learning this skill will improve your probability of success in a crowded market.

The Amazon Marketplace, as it exists today, is the most diverse and fair market there has been. Better still, we have a window into this market through book rank to evaluate success. Is it an entirely fair and level playing field? No; given that cumulative advantage is such a powerful force, new participants will never start on an equal footing. Will there be cheaters? Absolutely. There always has been and always will be. Will rank gravity suck more books into the abyss than cumulative advantage can push to profitability? Without a doubt!

That being said, history has shown that rank changes over time. New participants can capture that number one spot. Look at the holder of the most wealth in the world over recorded history[5]. The holder changes nearly every decade, and the new wealth typically comes from a source created by that person.

The right attitude, if you take part in the market, is one where you understand the role of talent, and how skill improvement leads to your success. The final variable – luck – is just that: circumstances out of your control[6]. Treat each book launch as a round you play, and in each round, you look to improve your cumulative advantage by showing your talent, applying your skill, and tilting probabilities to your advantage.

Now it's time to learn more about the two massive forces that are picking winners and losers in the market.

2
A CLASH OF TITANS

> *"Truth cannot be brought down; rather, the individual must make the effort to ascend to it. You cannot bring the mountaintop to the valley. If you would attain to the mountaintop, you must pass through the valley, climb the steeps, unafraid of the dangerous precipices."*
>
> — *JIDDU KRISHNAMURTI*

Trillions of individual choices make up the book market, culminating into two opposing forces: rank gravity and cumulative advantage. Rank gravity is such a powerful force that after the boost that Amazon's promotions provide, most books fall quickly out of view in the store. With no barriers to entry, anyone can publish a book on Amazon, adding mass to the pull of gravity.

The opposing force of rank gravity is cumulative advantage, and it drives a small selection of books to the top ranks, creating a skewed distribution. Cumulative advantage confounds classical economists because it refuses to follow the laws of supply and demand. Rather than supply and demand finding equilibrium, cumulative advantage propels a select few away from the masses in the long tail and delivers visibility and profit.

Cumulative advantage appears equally as harsh as rank gravity, maybe more so. Where rank gravity looks to pull all books into oblivion, cumulative advantage selects a favored few for all the rewards of rank heaven.

The problem is how do you harness it? It is like a landslide. A build-up of billions of individual particles, all acting on their own and somehow self-organizing into a massive, unstoppable force.

To understand how these two forces interact and conflict, let's begin with rank gravity.

IT'S NOT THE CLIFF, IT'S GRAVITY THAT KILLS YOU

The first force that you're fighting is supply. With an average of 88,000 new titles a month, there is no shortage of supply coming into the market. With no barriers to entry, expect that anyone with the inclination to write a book will, and they will get it published on Amazon.

If newly published titles were evenly spaced, you would face 2,933 titles launching the same day that you launch your book. But that's not the case; authors tend to launch toward the end of a month and on Fridays, so those days will have more launches. Traditional publishers have a launch season to take advantage of the holiday sales, thus concentrating more book launches in certain months. On any day, you're one of a thousand fresh salmon trying to swim upstream.

There is no reason to believe that there will be a limit to the number of titles released every year. As more courses teach the self-publishing process, more authors will try it.

I've been at conferences where a few authors have complained to me that the lack of gatekeepers is hurting the market, making it hard for consumers because they have to sort through the good and the bad. Those days of gatekeepers are gone. The market decides what authors merit getting paid for the stories they create.

Because of the lack of gatekeepers, a lot of uninteresting books get published. Those books get crushed in the black hole of rank gravity.

This is the downside of making sure that more creatives get a shot at finding an audience, and that means that more and more product will get put into the marketplace for the public to pick winners from.

THE BINGE ECONOMY

We live in a binge economy, and I have the data to prove it. I've been plotting title launches for authors I work with to understand performance. Plotting thousands of titles across genre and rank has revealed that an author's existing audience will consume a title's sales within three to four months of release.

The sales decay curve is essential to understand, as it is a part of the launch process. Rather than get bummed out when the data shows that your audience has burned through your latest book, see it as part of the cycle. The natural end of a season. Because average daily sales play such a large role in how Amazon ranks your book, the binge consumption of your existing audience creates a temporary lift off your rank plateau. You'll be well served by observing where it – and your other titles – remain after the launch.

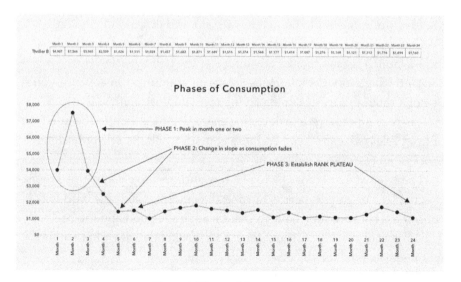

Figure 1: Phases of Consumption

After launch, the sales curve peaks in month one or two, depending on the day of the first month you launch the book. Many authors launch a book toward the end of the first month to recover preorder revenues sooner and to maximize page reads in the first month to trigger Kindle Unlimited bonuses. This creates a natural month-two peak in revenue.

From there, phase two begins, and a steep drop occurs through months three to six. The slope typically changes for another six months, then establishes a consumption plateau with far less decay. The tail becomes an indicator of how well we do with our marketing cycle and what the rank plateau will be for the title. Over time, we want to see the tail have a lift or stay level. A slowly building tail shows that we have offset the loss of older readers with new readers working through your backlist.

Below are examples from several genres. I show them normalized to US dollars per month. Using monthly sales normalizes sales (selling in a mix of countries, wide, or in Kindle Unlimited).

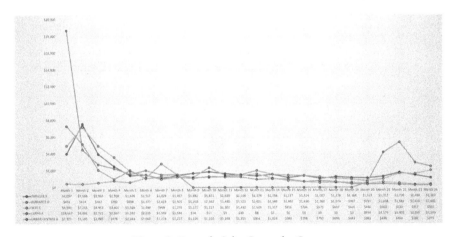

Figure 2: Example Sales Curves by Genre

Thriller B, Urban Fantasy A, and SCIFI C all follow the typical curve profile I showed in the previous illustration. The difference is that, in the case of Thriller B, it has a stable, rising tail. This is a good sign that you're adding audience over time.

LitRPG A is an example of a book that did very well in the initial phase, but then had no sales for months, until the second book launched in that series. This type of curve is common for books that are part of a series and not rapidly released.

Let me share an example from an author that is doing over one million a year in gross royalties on less than eight books a year. This author, like most I know or work with, doesn't achieve six or seven-figure revenues from publishing one book. The annual income is made up of a catalog of published works, with new titles every year.

This author continually worked on their craft and finally found the recipe for success; the right combination of voice, story, cover, and blurb to have a book take off. They marketed this book like the others, but it achieved a sub-100 rank in the store and held it for days. A few weeks later, the tails on previous books lifted. New readers were working their way through the backlist, increasing the sales for all the titles.

The chart below illustrates how over the life of the series books sales were influenced. On this chart I've separated the axis for the first book from the others to see the changes in book one sales with each launch (when on the same scale changes in book one is too small see). Book three began the progressive improvements of launch rank achievement and increased revenues.

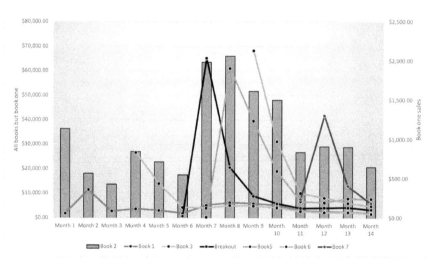

Figure 3: Romance Breakout Series

A few months later, the next book was released. This book achieved bestseller status with even better rank and more Kindle Unlimited bonuses. You can see that next peak at month seven, when this second bestseller took off.

With each launch of later books, you can see the upticks and new plateau setting. The first bestseller was momentous in this author's accumulation of advantage. It supercharged the business, lifting all titles and putting the author at a new level. Each launch since then has ratcheted up the business, meaning a vast audience stayed and read through old books. New books have a traditional decay profile, although they all have a higher rank plateau when they drop, showing cumulative advantage at work.

I convey this story not to get you focused on a rush to the top of the charts, but to show how this data helps you see customer behavior.

Below is a set of curves from different authors in the romance genre.

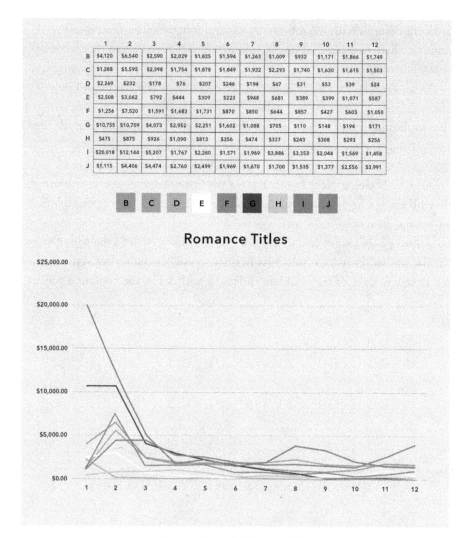

Figure 4: Example Romance Titles

The curves reflect various levels of success. As you can see, each of the curves has the same three slope changes. What differs is the intercept (month-one sales), then the slope changes in the different phases. You can also see that after the initial consumption, each book settles out to its plateau. This has to do with the individual book's rank, the size of the author's community, the number of books in the backlist, and the ranking of those books.

Here is a crucial mindset shift. Your book wasn't ascending the charts then had its momentum stolen by the evil Amazon algorithms; rather, it is that the rapid consumption by your existing audience gives your book a heightened rank that can't be sustained beyond the burst of consumption at launch. Your rocket doesn't have enough fuel (audience) to ascend higher, and you fall back to a lower orbit. Success is when your title gets to the third phase: it maintains a higher rank and lifts the ranks of your other titles.

I suggest taking your historical data and developing your own sales curves. Tracking monthly results across your titles will provide you with guidance about your performance. Gross sales are the number one indicator, but we are looking for a way to measure long-term audience addition. Producing a lot of books can keep your total sales level climbing, but what happens when you stop? Measuring the change in sales in a title over time will help you to see if an audience is reading through your backlist, and help you determine if you are adding or losing readers.

Having your baseline data helps you to see if you are leveling up after each launch cycle. While hitting a lower and lower rank with a book is exciting and should be celebrated, the real win is if, after the launch, all of your other titles have a lift that sustains.

To reiterate, high initial sales ranking is the interested audience you have already accumulated consuming the book. Then gravity takes over. The way to higher ranks is a bigger audience (duh!). The misconception is that you'll continue to build it during this launch.

In the optimal window of those first twenty-one days, when your existing audience is driving sales, that's when new readers are most likely to join. Your visibility is increased. After that, you'd do better to focus on retaining these new readers than hunting for more.

If you do advertise your books have you ever turned off your ads? Your rank would drop, as would your sales, but your profitability would improve. Try this and establish your organic audience attraction. This is the only way to determine if you're plowing money into ads with diminishing returns, an expensive symptom of a vicious marketing cycle. We need something more powerful than advertising and algorithms to overcome rank gravity. Something that makes your fuel tank bigger with each launch, setting you up to fly up to the next plateau of sales. That force is cumulative advantage.

ESTABLISHING A RANK PLATEAU

I have shown you examples where titles rebound to levels far above the original launch, but that was caused by some outside influence. I've observed this happening when an author cowrites with another "more famous" author. Readers then find the upstart author and begin reading through their backlist. Cowrites and anthologies can trigger this lift to rank as well. The best cause for this later lift is a breakout round where your book finally connects with a broader audience.

Outside of these "special" circumstances rank plateau changes happen in steps and slow ascents. The step changes are observed after a launch cycle. You need to be looking at sales curves over time to see slower ascents in your tail, where you are gradually adding more organic readers than losing them.

Once you have your breakout are you guaranteed to be top ranked? While cumulative advantage provides top authors with added help, it doesn't guarantee them a prime spot at all times. Keep in mind that while the top 100 books on Amazon will account for eighty percent of gross daily book revenues, those titles change hourly.

The top titles are fluid, and this is true now more than ever; it's been easier for indie or "breakout" titles to get to these lofty heights. You can't expect cumulative advantage and the virtuous marketing cycle to rocket a debut novel to the top 100 and stay there. This would be an unrealistic expectation. The aim is to use what you learn here to reach new rank heights with each launch, and establish higher rank plateaus.

A rank plateau is a floor you set where your books rank on average. This is your real rank, not the artificially high one that happens during launch. Your average rank outside of the launch window shows your resistance to rank gravity. While it is exciting to achieve a new top rank each cycle, your goal is to establish a higher plateau after the consumption cycle is over. The plateau represents your average daily earnings.

If you were to ascend Mount Everest, you wouldn't just start hiking up the mountain and continue on until you get to the top. You would likely die on the way up, or certainly die on the way down. The air at the top is rarified and requires acclimation. Expert climbers create basecamps to ascend from.

An ascent is made up of phases to acclimate to the thin air. Climbers go up to a slightly more difficult altitude, then they return to the safety of the base camp. When adapted, they move to the next base camp and then start another adaptation cycle. The right perspective of a launch isn't that you are being pulled away from your rightful rank at the top of the mountain, but that this is another cycle where you move your base camp up the mountain.

After reviewing my clients' data, I've observed either a consistent climb from launch to launch (the minority), or one breakout book that sets a new plateau, followed by higher plateaus but with less extreme rank changes. The breakout is driven by them finding their voice, and the story world finally resonating with an audience. It was by trying to understand how these authors could establish these plateaus that I saw the power of cumulative advantage and its inner workings.

Now let's get you a deeper understanding of what drives a few authors to prosper in such a crowded market.

3

WINNER TAKES ALL: UNDERSTANDING CUMULATIVE ADVANTAGE

> *"The truth is of course is that there is no journey. We are arriving and departing all at the same time."*
>
> — *DAVID BOWIE*

Picture a room of published authors. Let's pretend this is a cozy mystery conference. If you were to plot the authors' height on a chart, you would see a histogram in the shape of a bell. The graph would illustrate that the data collects around the average, tailing off toward a higher and lower extreme. The bell curve is a common distribution in nature and economics.

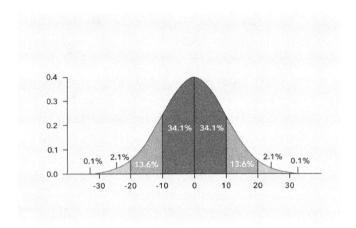

Figure 5: Standard Distribution

If the same group of authors plotted their income from book sales on a graph, you would not get a bell curve. Instead, you would see a right-skewed distribution, referred to as a Zipf curve, Pareto distribution, or J curve. The graph would follow a power law, showing that a few made most of the income. The winners takes all, well most.

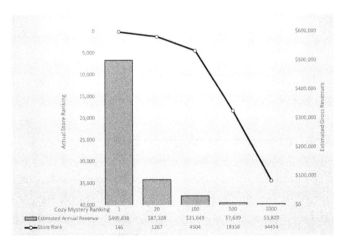

Figure 6: Revenue and Rank Curves for Cozy Mystery

In your hypothetical graph, would the author with the most revenue[1] also be the best educated, the most talented writer, and have the most literary awards? Most likely not. Nor would the case today be that that author would be with a large publisher. On the contrary, they may have been rejected hundreds of times by agents and editors.

If you crave to understand what is behind the success of best-selling authors and content producers, then you're not alone. It was in my quest to understand what drives creative content markets that I realized a complex force called cumulative advantage guides the results. It is the one force strong enough to overcome rank gravity.

R.K. Merton originally developed the term 'cumulative advantage' to explain the advancement of scientific careers.[2] There have been countless studies on how it drives market and social inequality. DiPrete and Eirich provide a comprehensive assessment of its application in the study of sociology, cataloging distributions, formulas, and theory as to its causality[3]. Frank and Cook also identify features inherent to winner-take-all markets.[4]

In my review of sources for this book, I found four predominant themes;

- research trying to predict winners
- confirmation of a specific distribution formula
- validation of cumulative advantage at work
- influence on fairness and equality

This book isn't a call for fairness, nor do I look to predict winners. If the force is a natural part of a market, then I wanted to learn how to use it to my advantage. Why try to swim upstream when there is such a strong natural current that can take you where you want to go?

What initially piqued my interest was seeing how various authors performed within the Amazon bookstore. In my work to help authors manage their business, marketing is always a topic of conversation. It has surprised me to see who succeeds and who doesn't. In short, it confounded me to see who the winners and losers were.

Was it based on talent? Some of the most successful authors were not what I would call talented. Was the issue a matter of taste? I didn't think so, and much of the research I read was focused on trying to predict winners. If talent and quality were the only determinants, it would be easy to know who would win and why.

Was it marketing acumen? As someone who sees behind the curtain of Amazon's top authors, there isn't one winning strategy. Instead, I saw success from conflicting strategies. I could point to authors doing well spending tens of thousands of dollars on advertising, as well as authors selling mid-six figures using no advertising. If there was a trend with the top authors, it was that advertising spend was lower than the industry average. Many of my clients didn't advertise, or their results crushed what advertising gurus were so proud of when trying to sell authors on their latest course.

There was something else at work, and no one had taken the time to understand it or try to harness its power. That force is cumulative advantage.

Cumulative advantage exists in any market where the current output creates resources or advantages that will influence future rounds.

There are economic, social, and psychological factors driving cumulative advantage. The winner does not take all immediately, but over time, they build up market share that can eventually become a monopoly. This winner-takes-all phenomenon isn't unique. We see it in the arts, entertainment, sports, finance, and the technology industry when a dominant technology overtakes competitors.

Understanding cumulative advantage and how it works will help you ride its powerful momentum up the ranks and build an audience. While this force has been researched and documented, little has been written on how to get it to work for you. That is what you'll learn here, but first you must understand its inner workings.

Let's revisit cumulative advantage in the game of Monopoly. In the game, all players start with the same amount of money and no property. The function of luck plays an enormous part; in the first few rounds, where you land determines the properties you will own. Chance delivers prime real estate to wheel and deal with in later rounds. Over time, you invest rent collected into new properties, or improvements on existing ones. This increases the probability of getting more renters and higher rent.

As the game progresses, a wider disparity between winners and losers develops. Winners can continue investing in improvements and holding cash to deal with the unfortunate luck of landing on competitive properties. At the same time, less fortunate players try to survive with fewer and fewer resources. In successive rounds, one lousy roll can put you out of the game, or give a lucky property owner added capital to scale up and wipe out competitors. In the end, someone owns the board.

In Monopoly, you can just let luck be the biggest driver of your success, or you can learn how the rules and structure of the game create ways to improve your advantage. For example, knowing the most landed-on properties and acquiring them – rather than looking to own the properties with the highest rent – will enhance the probability of winning.

Strong competitors with an advantage accumulate more power. We have seen this with technology companies, VHS dominated Betamax, Amazon beats out other online retailers. The difference in the actual world versus Monopoly is that all players don't start with the same resources, or on the same turn.

Does that mean that the game is rigged, and an unknown author or musician can never hold the number one position? Absolutely not!

While cumulative advantage tilts the playing field to the current winner, history has shown that new entrants can disrupt current leaders and take the pole position. This has happened even without understanding how these forces work. With a system that leverages and collects cumulative advantage, you will grow your business effortlessly. You can become a master of cumulative advantage by learning how similar power laws work in the economy and nature.

PAPA PARETO, THE FATHER OF POWER LAWS

Vilfredo Pareto is known for the 80/20 rule, typically called the Pareto Principle. If you're not familiar with the idea, it is the concept that eighty percent of the results come from only twenty percent of the causes.

This *"law of the vital few"* came from his research into income distribution. Pareto observed that eighty percent of the land in Italy was owned by twenty percent of the population.

The 80/20 rule is just one segment, or step, in a Pareto distribution, a curve that shows more accumulation of wealth by a select few. A Pareto distribution is a power law curve.

WHAT IS A POWER LAW?

Power laws are everywhere. George Zipf, a linguist, proved that in any language, there is an inverse proportion to the frequency of a word being used in that language.

For example, in English, *"the"* is the most commonly used word, and it occurs seven percent of the time in any writing. The next most often used word is *"of,"* used three-point-five percent of the time. Zipf's Law holds that each instance is the inverse square of the prior sample. Below is the Zipf's curve for the first 150,000 characters in this book.

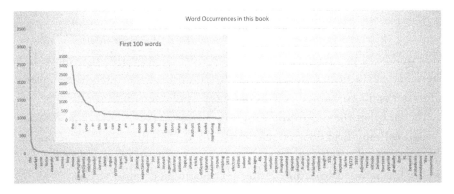

Figure 7: Zipf Analysis and graph of this book

Alfred Lotka observed a power law when looking at the frequency of publications, specifically in the matter of scientific papers and citations within scientific research. A small population produced most of the works.

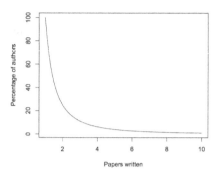

Figure 8: Example of a Lotka Distribution

In the case of the publishing industry, we see a power law in play, with two-point-four percent of authors earning sixty-five percent of the income.

These power laws are everywhere, and in some cases, compounding on themselves. Take the internet for instance; over time, there has been a winner-take-most result for the website with the highest traffic. While the number of people with access to the world wide web has exploded, there has never been a proportional distribution of website visits. Early adoption is no guarantee you'll hold a top spot over time, as evidenced by the fact that the top traffic spot has changed (AOL, Altavista, Yahoo, Google). Being first doesn't guarantee you'll keep the number one spot.

Albert et al. analyzed the structure of the web and found that the power law applied to 325,729 internet documents connected by 1,469,680 hypertext links.[5] "All these connections were characterized by the long-tail distribution described by Feldmann and Witt (1997). This example allows us to state again that a limited number of nodes have a high number of connections. On the other hand, a very large number of nodes have a limited number of connections."

Albert and his staff also calculated the so-called "diameter of the web" (i.e., the average distance between internet pages, determined by choosing two random pages and counting the number of clicks needed to move between them).[6] They found this diameter to be about nineteen clicks. What this means is that the whole internet operates under a power law, then power laws apply within the internet. Google rules search, Amazon rules e-commerce, and the list goes on.

Over time, the holder of the top website may shift, but the top-ranking sites will always gain more connections and traffic. This promotes helpful and harmful effects. Gaining cumulative advantage on the number one site of a category delivers faster aggregation of an audience. Gaining a ten-percent market share on the number two sales channel will be a fraction of one percent on the number one sales channel because the absolute customer size differentials are so large. Not that you should only focus on the number one player in a category, rather that its scale will influence what you can do within it.

Since our overall focus is on the reader, we should care about where we get the right readers, and not ignore platforms because fewer readers are using them. With smaller platforms, while the pool of potential readers is also smaller, it will take less to build an advantageous position on that platform. All of this is to say, where you develop your cumulative advantage will influence the scale and speed of the advantage you build.

Professional sports are another example where top players get a disproportionate amount of compensation based on rank. It takes a player time to move up into the ranks, then hold the position. A player can stay at the top for a lengthy period of their career, but eventually, physical performance wanes, and younger entrants take rank and its reward.

Recording artists also compete in a winner-take-most market. For decades, the market was fixed by record companies, but in 1991, music changed forever. This was when Billboard began using data rather than its honor and payola system for hit ranking.[7] Quickly, hip-hop and country gobbled up the top one hundred.[8]

This change in ranking also impacted which musicians were making the most money. Musical artists' financial success follows a Lotka distribution, where a few account for most of the revenues. Research by Cox, Felton, and Chung (1995) into the relationship between the number of gold records (an award for record sales), showed Lotka's law overestimates the earnings for one gold record, but underestimates the earnings for multiple gold records.[9] Just like in publishing we see that there are some self-organizing principles that get people to settle on a few popular artists.

WHERE DOES A BESTSELLER'S POWER COME FROM?

We have observed the power law distribution in the book market just like in the internet, sports and music. In a 2008 study analyzing point of sales data from 2,000 Japanese bookstores between April 2005 to March 2006, the research showed that the top 1.5% of titles controlled 47% to 52% of the market share. In this short but interesting paper, the researchers concluded that they understand the organization of a power-law-driven market (macroscopic level), was like other self-organizing natural events like earthquakes, avalanches, and the growth of cities. Takashi Iba posited that the observed power law curve was produced by consumers making their own product choices (microscopic level) with social feedback from friends and marketing influences that provided mesoscopic feedback.[10]

    The Amazon Kindle marketplace is cumulative advantage on steroids. More importantly, the marketplace is the Market. What do I mean? Amazon captures so much of the overall sales in the United States that while all sales don't go through them, enough do to make its ranking of fiction, non-fiction, and sub-genres statistically significant models of the entire book market. Regardless of what other bestseller lists say, the one true list is the Amazon Bestsellers list, as they base it on a larger, less arbitrary dataset.

    In November 2019, I helped a client with a launch for a book that reached number seven in the Amazon Kindle store. During the launch period, we tracked daily revenue from the book, a rolling average, and the number of books sold. We established an -0.85 correlation of rank to daily book sales.

    The chart below shows that book rank in the Amazon store follows a power law curve similar to those identified by Cox, Pareto, and others. Where $3,300 a day in sales achieved a rank of seven, it required at least $8,300 a day in sales to reach number one in the entire store during that same period.

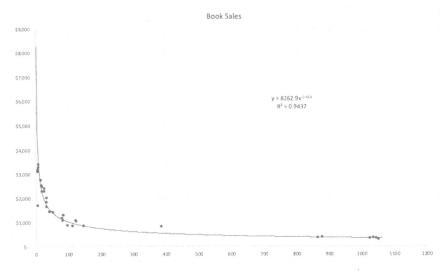

Figure 9: Power Law Curve Book Sales

Since then, I've consulted on several other launches that have reached the top twenty, then the book stayed in the top one hundred for at least two weeks. The numbers vary based on the mix of sales and competition, but I have validated the curve across different authors and genres.

There are a variety of web-scraping tools that provide projections for the number of book sales needed to reach a particular rank on Amazon. All show that exponential growth is required to achieve greater rank. Amazon's rank formula is mostly sales-driven, and while the exact amount of sales to reach the number one spot may change seasonally and over time, the immutable truth is that the ranking system is sales-volume-driven.

The reason I say that Amazon is cumulative advantage on steroids is that an enormous part of the marketing by Amazon on your behalf is driven by ranking and sales conversions. The authors and books that have clicks that turn into sales get more visibility. This formalizes the feedback loops mentioned by Iba in his research of the Japanese book market, automating and amplifying the promotion of current winners.

HOW DOES CUMULATIVE ADVANTAGE FORM?

Understanding how and why power laws form will deepen your knowledge of cumulative advantage. Let's use stock market investing as an example.

Imagine you are one of three investment fund managers. You all start with one hundred thousand dollars. At the end of the year, the S&P 500 (our performance benchmark) has increased by eight percent, your two competitors beat the S&P by two percentage points with a return of ten percent, and you delivered a twelve percent return. Purely from your talent as an investor, you have accumulated more wealth. You would have one-hundred-twelve thousand dollars, and your competitors, only one-hundred-ten thousand. At the end of the next year of investment, even if you were to deliver the same investment return as your competitor (10%), then you would have one-hundred-twenty-three thousand dollars to their one-hundred-twenty-one thousand dollars. Your advantage in round one continues to compound in later rounds, even if your performance regresses to the mean return of your competition.

However, if you were to continue your above-average performance for the first three rounds, at the end of round three, you would have one-hundred-forty thousand dollars, and your competition would only have one-hundred-thirty-three thousand dollars.

Do you see the compounding effect?

> *"For if person A can invest a dollar more efficiently than person B, person A can likely invest $1 billion better than person B and will end up controlling resources on a much larger scale. A small extra talent for control will command a large rent in the market equilibrium."*[11]

The compounding effect of your return each round on more and more cash (resources) will continue to build, but other factors come into play. As new investment comes into the market, these participants will be looking to make a good decision about who should manage their money. They will research and see that you are a better investor, and therefore you will attract a more significant percentage of new money coming into the market than your competitors. Now your return will apply to an even larger pool of resources, increasing your advantage. Next, your competition will lose investors as participants learn about your exceptional returns, and move their money to you, further accelerating the difference.

Now you have more customers, and when new entrants come into the market and seek personal recommendations by word of mouth, you have more referral points than your competitors, further seeding your fund collection. These referral points will advocate your mad investment skills because they associate a part of their own identity with your performance. In promoting you, they get to brag about how smart they are in choosing you.

Opportunity advantage now sprouts up. Because you are notorious and your opinion on investments is respected, people bring new ideas to you first. They want to be part of your success, and in doing so, you get to see opportunities before others. You now have a larger opportunity set earlier, if you choose to act on it.

Finally, when your resource pool is of a critical mass in the market, your actions will influence market results. An example being when you invest in a company, others will follow your lead, boosting your returns because you were there first.

Stock market investing is an obvious example, but you will discover as you read on that the principles are identical for building cumulative advantage in the consumption of your content.

How do you know if you're in a market driven by cumulative advantage? Look for the following characteristics:

Low reproduction cost: The producer can reproduce the original work and provide it at a reasonable price to the entire market. This is easy to understand in the digital era of music, books, and videos, but it is also true of athletes.
Professional leagues garner huge profits, and that money goes to the best teams and players because video transmission makes it easy for all to view the best of the best players.
Networks: When markets are made, or the product is more

valuable when greater numbers of consumers use the product, then the network standard commands cumulative advantage.[12]

Natural limits to the size of the agenda: We cannot or choose to keep track of a few options in a category. While we want freedom of choice, we don't want to spend too much effort on making that choice. This leads consumers to focus on the favored few.

Avoidance of Regret: Consumers don't want to make a poor choice and regret spending their money. Therefore, social proof and decisions made by others whose opinions matter to us will influence (or dictate) our choice. The adage 'No one ever got fired for choosing IBM' speaks directly to the avoidance of regret.

Position, aspiration, and bandwagon effects: When a product choice represents a part of our identity, such as the car we drive, the address we live at, or the clothes we wear, then top-ranking items take priority in our choice structure.

These characteristics are not always present, and sometimes it only takes one to create the conditions for cumulative advantage. If more than one, or all of the characteristics are present, then all the tears shed for the inequality of the market won't erode the monolithic force of cumulative advantage.

I hope you can see that the publishing market hits on all of these characteristics.

Economists have researched cumulative advantage for decades. It conflicts with classical theories of supply and demand because consumers choose a small selection of providers, rather than substituting equivalent products.

Before we dive deeper into recreating its effects, let's understand the causes.

SIZE AND SCALE

Gibrat's Law, sometimes called the rule of proportionate growth, was the work of Robert Gibrat in 1931. The law is like Zipf's Law, and states that a company's growth rate is proportional to its absolute size, and follows a power law curve. A 2015 study refuted the results, showing that there are varied growth rates across size and within size subsets.[13] While the biggest companies may have a broader opportunity set, purchasing power, and access to capital, sheer size alone is no guarantee that you will continue to accumulate advantage. Just like Monopoly, the actual world has disruptions from chance that can alter the economic landscape.

Observe the changes in the publishing world. When publishers were the conduit of published works, supply was limited to those providers, and their resources were significant, but their limited output never met demand. With the open-door policy of digital publishing, the supply of works has risen exponentially, and with this rise of new entrants, so has the distribution of wealth to smaller imprints and indie authors.

While the firm's absolute size may be a point of contention, having more resources and working capital always allows a business to scale faster. You may ask why the big publishers don't continue to dominate the industry, but a publisher's adherence to an old business strategy, or misapplication of those vast resources, can be out-maneuvered by nimble participants. Authors that earn more can out-advertise and out-market competitors, whether they be indie or traditional.

IS IT TALENT?

Rosen argued that the existence of superstars in a field is because of talent and first-mover advantage. In his research, he looked at musicians and singers, and how a small group commanded all the wealth. He postulated that unlike a classic labor market, where the price would find an equilibrium between supply and demand, the art market was different because the products were imperfect substitutes for each other. The buying public didn't want to pay less to hear a mediocre singer; rather, they would pay a higher price for the best. Rosen argues that a small set of superstars will dominate the market.[14]

Talent attracting a premium isn't a novel concept, nor is it hard to imagine why it takes place. If you have a health issue, you want the best doctor; legal problems, the best lawyer. I already walked you through talent in financial markets.

Rosen argued that with the addition of low cost, near-perfect reproduction of a performance, the talented artist has an advantage to exploit against other artists. From the demand side, reproduction allows consumers to get their demand met by the most talented artist. On the supply side, copy costs are near zero.

Rosen discussed the example of Elizabeth Billington, an opera singer popular in 1801, who, before the time of recording, earned over ten thousand pounds during the opera season. She might be more talented than Pavarotti, but she didn't have the modern singer's advantage of a low cost of reproduction coupled with global reach, so her fortunes were far smaller than Pavarotti's. Contemporary artists can scale to higher levels of wealth because a more significant market can find them and access them through low-cost reproduction.[15]

Adler takes a different view of how a star is born. In an equally talented pool of artists, they all have a similar chance. The selection of the superstar is luck-driven.[16] Consumers choose from the pool of talent, and each consumer's choice attracts similar consumers to do the same. The premise is that only a select group of talented people will get to be in this pool to begin with.

In some endeavors, this may be the case – certainly for sports, where genetics and athleticism play a part. However, for content creation, part of the talent may be in the ability to read the market and connect with an audience.

If you're an author, this is where sometimes the literary focus muddies the water. Being literary or artistic is one form of talent, but it may be difficult to commercialize. A talented pulp fiction writer can outsell a more talented literary writer. Each writer may be the top of the talent pyramid, but once you look to the marketplace as an arbiter, and revenue as the measuring stick, then what talent is valued more by the market?

Adler and Cox both observe that consumers reduce risk and acquisition costs when they can minimize search and learning costs.

There are other social implications from purchases. Amazon's product recommendations embody this research. Search results based on keywords are sales-weighted. Bestseller and popularity lists give further visibility to more audiences based on sales, thus leveraging cumulative advantage.

Most e-commerce systems provide you more of the same, or expose you to items that others with similar tastes have chosen via recommendation algorithms. On the surface, this is a beautiful thing. More and more products hit the market each day, and having help in making a choice reduces the cost of learning. However, it can also limit options, amplifying cumulative advantage.

Consumers derive further value in sharing what they know about the art with a community that appreciates the artist. Popular culture is based on a network effect commonly called fandom, where a participant can get further value out of a purchase through interaction with other fans. We will dive deeper into this in later chapters as, in my view, this fan community has more to do with success than talent.

Salganik, Dodds, and Watts (2008) created an experiment to test the impact of social influence on quality.

> *"One explanation for the observed inequality of outcomes is that the mapping from quality to success is convex (i.e., differences in quality correspond to larger differences in success), leading to what has been called the superstar effect, or winner-take-all markets. Because models of this type, however, assume that the mapping from quality to success is deterministic and that quality is known, they cannot account for the observed unpredictability of outcomes. An alternate explanation that accounts for both inequality and unpredictability asserts that individuals do not decide independently, but are influenced by the behavior of others."*[17]

In Watts' experiment, a group of 14,341 participants were asked to download and rate forty-eight unknown songs. Researchers randomly selected songs to rank as a control with no influence from other raters; they then put other subjects into eight independent, artificial cultural markets. In these artificial cultural markets, participants had knowledge of the number of downloads of other songs.

They ran two experiments: one where songs were presented randomly, arranged in a 16 x 3 rectangular grid (not ordered by download counts), and the second, where songs were presented in a single column ranked by the number of downloads. A song's rank became uncertain across these markets.

> *"Our results suggest not only that social influence contributes to inequality of outcomes in cultural markets, but that as individuals are subject to stronger forms of social influence, the collective outcomes will become increasingly unequal.[18]"*

The work shows the significant influence that knowledge of others' choices has on individual preference. "In general, the best songs never do very badly, and the worst songs never do extremely well, but almost any other result is possible[19]." Introducing the variable of a ranked presentation nearly tripled the uncertainty of results compared to the independent market. This experiment shows how the community component can deliver different results for equally talented authors.

A 2009 study tested Rosen and Adler's theories of superstars in markets where local content laws require resources to be spent to increase cultural consumption of local languages.[20] Researchers found that the legislation to increase sales for Basque and Catalan musicians increased music diversity in consumers prepared to commit resources to doing further research. The two studies show that perceptions of quality and individual choice are influenced by social aspects of selection and market diversity.

In my investigation, I see an interesting intersection of network design, sociology, and psychology that I believe influences cumulative advantage. The trigger for me was a simple diagram in Iba's study of the Japanese book market[21]. The illustration shows how individual behavior at the microscopic level builds to consumer behavior at the mesoscopic level, promoting cumulative advantage at the macroscopic level. The macro effect then feeds back on the individual behavior of others. They call this concept self-organizing criticality of sales in a product market. Below is Iba's illustration. Dr. Iba has graciously provided permission for its reproduction in this book.

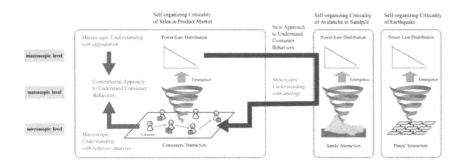

Figure 10: New approach to understanding market and consumer's behavior

If you agree with me that there is some self-organizing feedback that builds, then it is feasible to guide that organization. If social interaction and behavior drive cumulative advantage and create a positive feedback loop, why couldn't you build a system that promotes cumulative advantage? Initially, you may mistake social media, digital connectedness, search engines, and algorithms that amplify advantage as being the whole of that system. But none of these systemically create favorable conditions for cumulative advantage, and some may damage networks trying to produce it.

WILL THIS SYSTEM GUARANTEE YOU WILL BECOME A BESTSELLER?

The most concerning fallacy about success is that with digital publishing and the elimination of gatekeepers, passive income is now in your reach, and indie writers have been raking in cash. The number of millionaire authors has indeed increased, but so has the percentage of authors that haven't made more than $10,000 in their lifetime. Success rates haven't changed; only the population of authors has. There are some basics you must have, and if you have these, then the system will improve your advantage.

You need to be a capable writer: Most authors who struggle to sell books are just not interesting storytellers. No amount of marketing and advertising will get an audience to come back for more. In this same category goes product quality, meaning an eye-catching book cover and a well-edited book. Without a good story, genre-appropriate cover, and solid editing, your product will be seen as sub-standard.

Patience: You need to be prepared to wait while cumulative advantage builds; it requires time for the accumulation. This also means having the working capital to last through early unprofitable launches while you build your audience. Remember, the basis of cumulative advantage is using resources from past rounds in future rounds. You have to participate in multiple rounds to use the resources you have accumulated.

Audience Interaction: Some authors don't see audience development and interaction as part of the job description. This attitude and ensuing resistance amount to swimming against the current of cumulative advantage.

If you can't address the items above, then what I have put together won't help. If you have already found a measure of success, are in this for the long haul, and are willing to show your readers some love and respect, then you have the foundation.

The following chapters share some foundational concepts that are the basis for the system, including the supporting research. After that, we will go another layer deeper to unravel the workings of the system. I will illustrate how, over time, you can increase your probability of getting cumulative advantage to do your heavy lifting, just like knowing how to use the rules and probabilities of Monopoly improves your chances of winning. Understand that the preparation work has a compounding effect

An interesting revelation that I've had while working with clients is that advertising has diminishing returns and plateaus. Unless we combine it with the practices that foster cumulative advantage, your advertising won't scale. Yes, even authors spending tens of thousands of dollars on advertising see diminishing returns and need to leverage their audience.

Conversely, I work with authors that do high six to seven figures that spend nothing on advertising. They have successfully built systems that perpetuate cumulative advantage.

As of this writing, the top three authors on Amazon are JK Rowling, Dean Koontz, and Andrzej Sapkowski. The first holds this position without writing a recent book in her flagship series for years, and moves in and out of the number one spot. She builds cumulative advantage because her audience is so big that it literally perpetuates itself. Original readers of her books introduce their offspring to the stories in the form of books or movies.

Andrzej Sapkowski is a superb example of an author with a successful following that many envy, yet he was much further down in overall rank than the top 100 until he built more audience with the success of the Netflix adaptation of his series.

An authentic example of cumulative advantage creating greater opportunity. Earlier rounds created the advantage that facilitated video game makers to reach out to him to license the book content. The success of the games built his audience further and led to the Netflix series offer. This round opened up his work to a new audience in a different medium, reinvigorating his book sales to the point of getting him to the number three rank. In future rounds, he will build more advantage as he releases more books, or new seasons release on Netflix.

More often than not, the number one paid book on Kindle is penned by an indie author. Someone who, in the past, would have been shut out of the market. They are likely a ten-year overnight success, now raking in six figures a month in sales because they have put in countless hours writing outstanding books and connecting with their fans.

So how do we get you to stand out from your peers? Dive into the next chapter, and learn about how recognition and popularity are intertwined with cumulative advantage.

4

IS THERE A FORMULA FOR RECOGNITION AND POPULARITY?

> *The ideals which have always shone before me and filled me with the joy of living are goodness, beauty, and truth.*
>
> — *ALBERT EINSTEIN*

Do you recognize anyone in the picture?

Figure 11: 1927 Solvay Conference

For most people, the face that will pop out is the one just to the right of center, Albert Einstein.

This picture is from the 1927 Solvay Conference, an annual gathering of leaders in scientific thought This group is responsible for over seventeen Nobel prizes. If you're a physics nerd, you may have recognized more faces, and would be prepared to argue that when it comes to actual scientific contribution, others in the picture are more intellectually talented than Einstein. But Einstein will be the most recognized face by a large margin.

Few would recognize Niels Bohr, or that two seats to Einstein's right is Marie Curie (winner of two Nobel prizes in separate categories), or that she sits to the left of Max Planck. In the middle of the back row in the light-colored coat is Erwin Schrödinger (without his cat). Three people to his left is Werner Heisenberg; *Breaking Bad* fans will recognize the name as Walter White's meth-cooking alter ego.

In a group of the most talented physicists in the twentieth century, a scientific dream team, Einstein is the one we recognize. Why don't we recognize all of these scientists equally or based on merit? Why is it that some in a field become more notorious, and other talented people never get recognized?

The visual image of Einstein triggers bundles of neurons that release chemicals in your brain. Those neurons don't bring up a copy of his Wikipedia page, citations from a book, or a copy of a movie you saw. The ipicture triggers an electron charged neurotransmitter soup in a section of your brain, activating associations, memories, feelings, and learning – your Einstein. You feel a level of satisfaction in recognizing him, and you understand the idea of Einstein at an unconscious level. If I asked you questions about him, you would access other memories associated with the concept of Einstein, tapping into your long-term memory to extract facts.

You have an intellectual understanding that all the people in the picture are smart and have made significant contributions to the fields of science. But with Einstein, there is an emotional connection. For many, he has become the most recognizable symbol of free-spirited genius. You may have a much deeper understanding of his research and the theory of relativity, but few have ever read those works. Your Einstein and mine aren't the same. While we both recognize his picture, or his name in print, what Einstein is to you is your collection of associations. It is highly probable that you never met Einstein, so all of your associations are from indirect experiences, like reading or watching a show. If Einstein has become an icon of free-spirited genius for you, then that is a story you created in your head. The archetype associated with his likeness is a fabrication.

Let's talk about another Nobel laureate, Daniel Kahneman. He was awarded the prize for his work in economics, the specific contribution being;

> *"Integrated economic analysis with fundamental insights from cognitive psychology, in particular regarding behavior under uncertainty, laying the foundation for a fresh field of research."*[1]

That is a fancy way of saying that Kahneman and his long-time partner Amos Tversky are the founding fathers of behavioral economics.

They looked at how psychology influences our decision-making when we face uncertainty.

Kahneman's book *Thinking Fast and Slow* is a synthesis of years of research. If you want to understand how irrational we are, I highly recommend reading his book.

One of Kahneman's ideas is that of 'the experiencing self' and 'the remembering self'. The remembering self is the one that attaches meaning to what our experiencing self goes through. Most of what we experience either never leaves the unconscious, or doesn't warrant being remembered. It is the remembering self that filters and processes the information and tells us the story of what we experienced.

Think about Batman. What comes to mind? Is it the campy Batman of the sixties TV show, the Dark Knight of Chris Nolan or Frank Miller? If it is the Batman of Chris Nolan's movie, do you think of that character separate from the actor Christian Bale? This is all up in your head. The perception you have of the character, story, and the actor are all colored with your memory and association. In this example, your thoughts of Batman and mine will be more divergent because there have been so many different symbols and stories of Batman. All your Batman experiences get synthesized by your remembering self.

Let's go back to my Einstein example. How is it that Einstein developed into this brand for genius? Was he just so exceptional that we all came to the same conclusion?

Would you agree with the following statement?

> *"Albert Einstein is one of the most famous, iconic, influential, and universally admired persons in human history."*[2]

If you agreed, then you can thank a company called Greenlight and the University of Jerusalem. They are responsible for creating the idea of Einstein. The quote is the opening statement on the licensing website for Albert Einstein.

The website then declares,

> *"The names 'ALBERT EINSTEIN' and 'EINSTEIN' and the official Albert Einstein logos are either trademarks or registered*

trademarks belonging to the Hebrew University of Jerusalem. Any rights associated with Albert Einstein, including creations, appellations, copyrights, rights of publicity, photographs, trademarks, and characterizations, may not be used without permission from the Hebrew University of Jerusalem. Represented by Greenlight, a part of Branded Entertainment Network."[3]

Greenlight represents dozens of deceased persons who we readily accept as icons without thinking there may have been a strategy in place to create common messaging and cultural fluency.

Let me list a few of their clients, along with the tagline they've created for these icons.

Film Legend - Charlie Chaplin *is one of the most beloved and recognizable screen legends of all time. Best known for his role as the Little Tramp, he personifies humor, resilience, and individualism — attributes that make him relevant today.*

The King - Elvis Presley *is one of the most celebrated and beloved musicians and performers of all time. His status today as a legendary icon is unparalleled… the voice and the image of The King are forever ingrained in American pop-culture.*

Blonde Bombshell - Marilyn Monroe *Marilyn's timeless appeal and cultural impact continue to inspire fans around the world. Musicians, writers, and artists have celebrated her extraordinary character. Truly one of the most glamorous and recognizable women of the 20th century, she sets the standard for sex appeal and beauty.*

The King of Cool - Steve McQueen *"The King of Cool" was the ultimate man's man, admired by men, loved by beautiful women, and captured by the world's top photographers. Hollywood legend, motorsports hero, and cultural icon, McQueen rose to heights of fame that few others have achieved.*

The Voice of a Generation - Dr. Martin Luther King, Jr. *was an inspirational minister, powerful visionary, and leader of the American civil rights movement. A passionate speaker with the ability to truly move people, Dr. King is an enduring symbol of nonviolent activism and social justice.*[4]

In the case of Elvis Presley, the estate has been more profitable than while the King was alive. Revenues have continued to grow, with earnings of forty million dollars in 2018. Marylin Monroe's estate earned fourteen million in the same year. In both cases, the ghosts outperformed their living counterpart in revenue production.

Greenlight and other good marketers use behavioral psychology to create patterns that you can easily recognize, which can then help you interpret the message. You could say they brainwash us. I suggest that they are just using behavioral psychology to get our unconscious working for them. They leverage mental shortcuts, pattern creation, and matching to get us to come to a collective meaning for an icon. This makes it easy to recognize and create shared meaning in society. It takes a concerted effort to do this, but when it is done well, these imprints on our unconscious create a collective meaning and archetype.

We have a compulsion to attach meaning and use stories to understand situations. We create the symbolism around the symbol. Human givens, Jungian psychology, and Joseph Campbell's work all infer that story and metaphor are part of our unconscious and tap into familiar primal and spiritual stories.

What do you want readers to recognize? Your characters, you, a brand? Think through what you want to embed in their neural pathways, the meaning and iconography that you want to endure. Regardless of the icons of your work, it will take time and repeated effort to create the meaning and to grow the popularity. It won't come spontaneously. If you want your books or brand to pop out like Einstein's face did from equally smart people, you need to work on getting that recognition and popularity, like the University of Jerusalem did by hiring Greenlight.

WHAT WILL IT TAKE TO MAKE YOUR BRAND OR BOOKS AS ICONIC AS ALBERT EINSTEIN?

While Einstein was an actual person, he is now dead, so what exists is the *character* of Einstein. Those with a commercial interest are using his likeness for profit.

As an author, you can do the same with your characters. There is no difference between the Einstein in my head and one of your story's characters. Both are a collection of neuron pathways and chemical interactions that I recall from the experience of reading or watching a movie.

> *Your characters and story world exist in this same unconscious space that influences a reader's choice and decision-making.*

Just like your associations with Einstein, a reader unconsciously creates associations, but without a deliberate plan, those associations will be more like Batman rather than Einstein.

Kahneman also has done extensive research on recognition. Recognition comes from the ability to pattern match easily. This goes back to how our primal brain works (more on this later). By using strategies to create the patterns and associations you want a reader to have about your characters and story, you create common meaning. This work is done at the individual level, or what I call the neuroscopic level. As you read that part of the book, you will learn the tools you have at your disposal to create shared meaning and emotional connection with readers.

There is more to building cumulative advantage, a lot more, but purposefully creating an emotional connection between your readers and your story world is the main hook. As we go deeper, you'll understand just how to do this. However, there is another part you need to familiarize yourself with, and that is getting individuals to take the personal connection to your brand to the level of social convention. How do we do that? Fads and trends are so mysterious in their formation. Is it all luck?

In the next chapter, I'll share research that shows what is behind the creation of social convention.

5

SAY MY NAME: HOW TRENDS DEVELOP AND WHY IT'S IMPORTANT TO YOU

> *"Marilyn Monroe wasn't even her real name, Charles Manson isn't his real name, and now, I'm taking that to be my real name. But what's real? You can't find the truth, you just pick the lie you like the best."*
>
> — *MARILYN MANSON*

What's your name? If you're a female in the United States of America, and were born between the years of 1970 and 1984, there is a high probability your name is Jennifer. You may have a grandmother named Mary.

I'm not a psychic or talking to your dead relatives. I'm just observing trends created from naming conventions. During those years, Jennifer was the number one name chosen for newborn females according to Social Security data. And Mary was the dominant name for females for almost one hundred years.

These trends are what psychics use to cold-read a room, knowing that in a predominantly female audience, they will trigger someone with the names Mary and Jennifer.

Names are an excellent example of social convention. They play an essential role in how we are seen, both as an individual and as part of society. Our parents want to select an identifier that is individual, yet signals that we are part of a group or groups — groups that span a spectrum of geography, religion, ethnicity, and other social categories.

Below is a graphic representation from BabyNameWizard.com that shows the number of babies per million with a particular female name. You can see the changes over time and how there has been a shift away from a few names to a more diverse set of names.

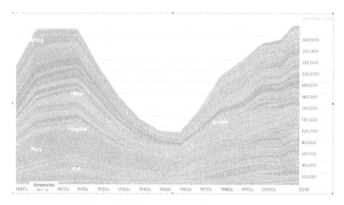

Figure 12: Female names last 100 years

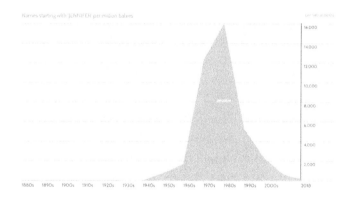

Figure 13: Jennifer's rise in popularity

The name Jennifer reached its zenith in the 80s after being one of the most popular names for twenty-five years.

These same societal structures that create a popular name out of nothing can help us understand how a social convention develops. We can see these trends when we look at the naming data from U.S. Social Security for the past one hundred years. There are trends where names move in and out of fashion and jockey for the top positions.

What is it that causes these names to trend up in popularity?

Opinions vary on why there has been a shift in naming conventions. Some believe it is to signal individuality; others attribute it to cultural diversity or the influence of popular culture.

This chapter isn't about untangling naming conventions. Instead, name choice is a way to understand how *individual* decisions coalesce into a *societal* trend. As an author, you seek common social conventions about your brand and story experience. The selection of a name has lifelong implications and has no economic cost; you can pick any name, and there is no financial benefit or loss.

How is it that millions of strangers making permanent personal choices about names cause multiple-year trends of the same names being selected, and a few names being so popular?

A NIECE NAMED EMMA

When we heard that my had in-laws named their daughter Emma, my wife and I asked if they knew how popular that name had become. They were living in Mexico at the time, and we wondered if they knew how many parents had selected the same name for a daughter. They didn't know, but the reason for their choice was it was the same in Spanish and English.

The interesting thing about the name Emma is it's not new. Nor is it as popular as it has been. In fact, the current population of Emmas is much smaller than that of the late nineteenth century.

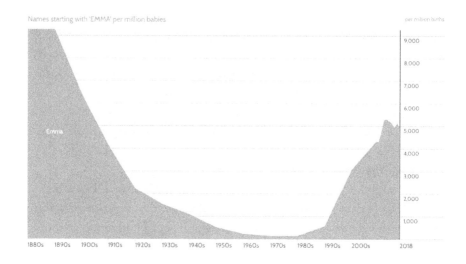

Figure 14: Emma popularity 100 years

Below is a table of the top five male and female names last forty years. Clear multi-year trends occur, with a handful of names jockeying for the top positions.

Year	Rank 1	Rank 2	Rank 3	Rank 4	Rank 5
2018	Emma	Olivia	Ava	Isabella	Sophia
2017	Emma	Olivia	Ava	Isabella	Sophia
2016	Emma	Olivia	Ava	Sophia	Isabella
2015	Emma	Olivia	Sophia	Ava	Isabella
2014	Emma	Olivia	Sophia	Isabella	Ava
2013	Sophia	Emma	Olivia	Isabella	Ava
2012	Sophia	Emma	Isabella	Olivia	Ava
2011	Sophia	Isabella	Emma	Olivia	Ava
2010	Isabella	Sophia	Emma	Olivia	Ava
2009	Isabella	Emma	Olivia	Sophia	Ava
2008	Emma	Isabella	Emily	Olivia	Ava
2007	Emily	Isabella	Emma	Ava	Madison
2006	Emily	Emma	Madison	Isabella	Ava
2005	Emily	Emma	Madison	Abigail	Olivia
2004	Emily	Emma	Madison	Olivia	Hannah
2003	Emily	Emma	Madison	Hannah	Olivia
2002	Emily	Madison	Hannah	Emma	Alexis
2001	Emily	Madison	Hannah	Ashley	Alexis
2000	Emily	Hannah	Madison	Ashley	Sarah
1999	Emily	Hannah	Alexis	Sarah	Samantha
1998	Emily	Hannah	Samantha	Sarah	Ashley
1997	Emily	Jessica	Ashley	Sarah	Hannah
1996	Emily	Jessica	Ashley	Sarah	Samantha
1995	Jessica	Ashley	Emily	Samantha	Sarah
1994	Jessica	Ashley	Emily	Samantha	Sarah
1993	Jessica	Ashley	Sarah	Samantha	Emily
1992	Ashley	Jessica	Amanda	Brittany	Sarah
1991	Ashley	Jessica	Brittany	Amanda	Samantha
1990	Jessica	Ashley	Brittany	Amanda	Samantha
1989	Jessica	Ashley	Brittany	Amanda	Sarah
1988	Jessica	Ashley	Amanda	Sarah	Jennifer
1987	Jessica	Ashley	Amanda	Jennifer	Sarah
1986	Jessica	Ashley	Amanda	Jennifer	Sarah
1985	Jessica	Ashley	Jennifer	Amanda	Sarah
1984	Jennifer	Jessica	Ashley	Amanda	Sarah
1983	Jennifer	Jessica	Amanda	Ashley	Sarah
1982	Jennifer	Jessica	Amanda	Sarah	Melissa
1981	Jennifer	Jessica	Amanda	Sarah	Melissa
1980	Jennifer	Amanda	Jessica	Melissa	Sarah
1979	Jennifer	Melissa	Amanda	Jessica	Amy
1978	Jennifer	Melissa	Jessica	Amy	Heather

Table 1: Female names 1978-2018

	Rank 1	Rank 2	Rank 3	Rank 4	Rank 5
2018	Liam	Noah	William	James	Oliver
2017	Liam	Noah	William	James	Logan
2016	Noah	Liam	William	Mason	James
2015	Noah	Liam	Mason	Jacob	William
2014	Noah	Liam	Mason	Jacob	William
2013	Noah	Jacob	Liam	Mason	William
2012	Jacob	Mason	Ethan	Noah	William
2011	Jacob	Mason	William	Jayden	Noah
2010	Jacob	Ethan	Michael	Jayden	William
2009	Jacob	Ethan	Michael	Alexander	William
2008	Jacob	Michael	Ethan	Joshua	Daniel
2007	Jacob	Michael	Ethan	Joshua	Daniel
2006	Jacob	Michael	Joshua	Ethan	Matthew
2005	Jacob	Michael	Joshua	Matthew	Ethan
2004	Jacob	Michael	Joshua	Matthew	Ethan
2003	Jacob	Michael	Joshua	Matthew	Andrew
2002	Jacob	Michael	Joshua	Matthew	Ethan
2001	Jacob	Michael	Matthew	Joshua	Christopher
2000	Jacob	Michael	Matthew	Joshua	Christopher
1999	Jacob	Michael	Matthew	Joshua	Nicholas
1998	Michael	Jacob	Matthew	Joshua	Christopher
1997	Michael	Jacob	Matthew	Christopher	Joshua
1996	Michael	Matthew	Jacob	Christopher	Joshua
1995	Michael	Matthew	Christopher	Jacob	Joshua
1994	Michael	Christopher	Matthew	Joshua	Tyler
1993	Michael	Christopher	Matthew	Joshua	Tyler
1992	Michael	Christopher	Matthew	Joshua	Andrew
1991	Michael	Christopher	Matthew	Joshua	Andrew
1990	Michael	Christopher	Matthew	Joshua	Daniel
1989	Michael	Christopher	Matthew	Joshua	David
1988	Michael	Christopher	Matthew	Joshua	Andrew
1987	Michael	Christopher	Matthew	Joshua	David
1986	Michael	Christopher	Matthew	Joshua	David
1985	Michael	Christopher	Matthew	Joshua	Daniel
1984	Michael	Christopher	Matthew	Joshua	David
1983	Michael	Christopher	Matthew	David	Joshua
1982	Michael	Christopher	Matthew	Jason	David
1981	Michael	Christopher	Matthew	Jason	David
1980	Michael	Christopher	Jason	David	James
1979	Michael	Christopher	Jason	David	James
1978	Michael	Jason	Christopher	David	James

Table 2: Male names 1978-2018

POPULAR CULTURE

Is this all just a matter of popular culture? Popular culture plays a part in making trends, in that popularity begets popularity.

The name Bella peaked at #58 in 2009, and one reason may have been the *Twilight* movie being released in 2008. After a slight loss in popularity, it has again peaked, and remains in the top one hundred female name choices.

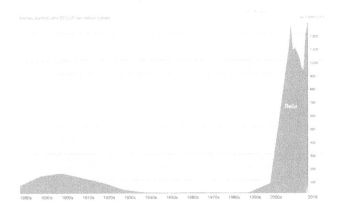

Figure 15: Bella name popularity

In 2009, the number of girls named Arya trended up. At the time, *Game of Thrones* was showing on HBO, and its character Arya Stark gained a larger share of the collective consciousness.

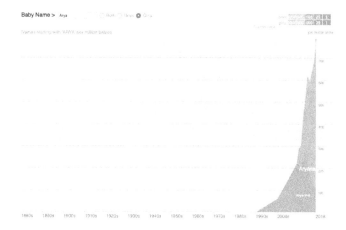

Figure 16: Arya name popularity

Large cultural movements can influence name choice. Some select a name because of a movie. They have an emotional connection to the character (yes, character connection can be so intense, you name your offspring after a fictional person), or it can be a matter of availability. The availability heuristic heavily influences us, and while not caught by our conscious brain, our unconscious has registered the name.

Naming conventions in the late twentieth century and early twenty-first century look to balance individuality and societal acceptance. This influences some parents to move away from one group of names and gravitate to a new grouping of names to be unique.

However, they are also influenced by a need for the identifier to meet with social convention. We don't want our child to have issues in the community because of how others judge their name. But how does it happen that our cool, unique but accepted name is trending with other parents?

Understanding how naming trends work is important, as it similar to the social conventions of choosing what types of games we play, the movies we watch, and the books we read.

INVISIBLE FORCES

Populations can produce linguistic conventions on popular names for children and pets, on common names for colors, and on popular terms for novel cultural artifacts, such as referring to junk email as "spam". Similarly, economic conventions such as bartering systems, beliefs about fairness, and consensus regarding the exchangeability of goods and services, emerge with clear and widespread agreement within communities, yet vary broadly across them.[1]

It is as if there is some invisible force, some magnetism that attracts us to specific trends. This is different than an information cascade, where a single piece of information is passed along. This is classic virality where I tell you the score of a game, and now that you know, you can tell others. Virality differs from the development of a social convention like name selection.

Centrola and Baronchelli conducted experiments to understand how social conventions develop. How is it that spam became the nomenclature for unwanted emails? These conventions – be it words we use, beliefs we hold, or value for goods exchanged – get widespread agreement with no centralized authority.

Centrola and Baronchelli ran an experiment in which they would show the participants a baby's face, and then the subjects would select an appropriate name for the baby. The researchers paired subjects each round, and if both picked the same name, they rewarded the winners fifty cents; if you didn't, you would have fifty cents deducted from your account. To avoid pre-existing popularity of names, they gave the participants an arbitrary list of ten names in random order at the beginning of the experiment.[2]

They ran this game in three types of networks: a spatial network (diagram A), a random network (diagram B), and a homogenous network (diagram C). A spatial network has strong connections to neighbors and no weak connections across the network. Each neighbor has several strong connections to nearby neighbors, known as a wide bridge. A random network has a combination of strong neighbor links and weak links across the network, and the homogenous network has every member with the same type of connection.

Figure 17: Three Network Models

In the first two networks, it took longer to establish common naming conventions, and once established, there were defined groups that collaborated better than others. The homogenous group learned the conventions slower, but eventually worked as one group.[3]

The results proved that spontaneous social conventions develop naturally. Network connections and structure influenced the time it took for the social agreement to form. In the homogenous network, the entire network quickly grew to a specific choice for all baby-naming. In the other two networks, a common answer never swept the network. Cells within the network developed, meaning there wasn't total consensus, but tribal consensus.

The power of social convention development lies in the network of people supporting the idea. Getting the network right promotes individual connection and communication. Just like independent baby name choices develop into cultural trends, the personal choices of customers roll up to cultural trends.

There are forces at play that we can channel to your benefit. If scientists can get social convention to form in a name-picking marketplace, why can't we use this learning to create social convention around your brand? The beauty is that the forces that create convention will be further amplified by the mechanisms that Amazon uses to help customers find what is trending and popular.

IS FANATICISM THE WAY TO CONVERT A SOCIETY?

Centrola conducted another experiment called the 'Emperor's Dilemma'. It based the experiment on the Hans Christian Andersen fable. In the story two swindlers pose as tailors come to town to make clothes for the emperor. The emperor spends lavishly on clothes. They tell emperor and his court that the cloth they will weave will appear invisible to the stupid and incompetent. The emperor, his court and the town all play along for fear of being labeled a fool. The ruse is foiled when a child calls out that the emperor has no clothes.

> *"In this model, agents must decide whether to comply with and enforce a norm that is supported by a few fanatics and opposed by the vast majority. They find that cascades of self-reinforcing support for a highly unpopular norm cannot occur in a fully connected social network. However, if agents' horizons are limited to immediate neighbors, highly unpopular norms can emerge locally and then spread. One might expect these cascades to be more likely as the number of 'true believers' increases, and bridge ties are created between otherwise distant actors."* [4]

The authors observed quite the opposite effects. Within the crowd, there is collective intelligence, or a larger organism that we need to influence. Having rabid fans won't start a cascade of fans without the right network conditions and behavior change. Your fans could be seen as the few fanatics with the wrong idea (the tailors).

Centrola's work shows that an enormous part of getting a fan base to grow requires understanding the structure of the underlying social network. Certain networks are better at conducting information, and others at reinforcing that information. You will need to build a community that transmits and strengthens the social convention that your brand is the obvious choice.

Creating a bias toward your work and nurturing group dynamics to build and reinforce consensus takes far more than just posts about your brand. But if Dr. Centrola can get strangers in an online network to agree on common names for a baby, we can design a system that reinforces the messaging that you want around your brand and books.

We are looking to build an audience for our books where they reinforce each other's decision that your books are good and that the shared experience in the community is even better. For your fans to be a community and to communicate and collaborate, there needs to be a universal language and agreement on the meaning of the brand. Just like Greenlight has established a common idea of Einstein as the free-spirited genius. When you provide a cohesive message, your community can agree on what your brand delivers.

Thus, the next step down in this layer is brand.

THE MESOSCOPIC LAYER

Where Cumulative Advantage is Aggregated

6
YOUR BRAND

> "*All fixed set patterns are incapable of adaptability or pliability. The truth is outside of all fixed patterns.*"
>
> — BRUCE LEE

A properly constructed mesoscopic layer has two elements: your brand and your community. Brand and community are synergistic. Your brand is the common language and the unifier. It attracts readers to the community and communicates what it will do for the consumer. Community allows members to meaningfully associate with the brand and others like them. This community becomes a reinforcement mechanism and a support structure. Once it comes to life, it will naturally look to grow, as all living organisms do.

Let's begin by discussing brand.

I offer a fresh approach to brand. We won't be discussing logotypes or looks; instead, I will draw from two areas, social psychology and religion, to illustrate how brand is far more than just a logo or common-themed book covers.

Think of your favorite brands; you can identify them, but more importantly, you identify *with* them. A brand helps people identify what your product is all about and what to expect.

You see, while it is important to create brand identity, it is more important to create a way for your readers to take on that identity and associate with it. When done correctly, their personal identity will in some way be defined by your brand, making them de facto representatives.

Think of how your personal identity has been influenced by brands. Sure, it can be the clothes you wear or the car you drive, but what about quotes from movies you've memorized, or your favorite books? Star Wars, Marvel, Harry Potter, and Star Trek are just a few that influence the identity of their fans.

If the key component of cumulative advantage is the accumulation of fans, then we need something for them to aggregate around. Your brand gives them the common theme to support or, better still, see as part of themselves. It is the magnet that attracts them and the glue that holds them together.

In later chapters, I'll cover practices to deliver an emotional connection between the reader and your brand, but before we get into the actionable steps, you'll be exposed to further information that reveals what makes a brand compelling.

WHERE DOES YOUR BRAND COME FROM?

One of the first decisions you need to make is what will anchor your brand. Will it be your author personality, or the series and characters? These are not mutually exclusive; you can focus on both. But your choice will determine how you craft your brand.

Many authors are hesitant to let the brand build around themselves. They don't like the attention. If you noticed in the paragraph above, I said your 'author personality'. You can create your author persona just like you do a character.

No matter how you see yourself, the level of introversion you feel, or your social awkwardness, your readers don't see you that way. They have an emotional attachment to your creativity through story and character. Their perception of you differs from reality, and the more you work to craft that persona, the better it will support your brand.

I've found that few authors use their characters and story world to drive brand. As an author, you are a natural at creating an interesting story, and rather than keeping your story world out of reality, you must blur the lines between the two.

This should also change how you think of advertising, as you focus less on copy trying to convert, and more on what you and your readers love – i.e., characters and story.

Popular culture is unique; we build emotional relationships with the imaginary. The para-social relationships your fans develop with your characters (more on this in later chapters) can be your most powerful sales tool. Your fans' imaginary relationship with the object of their fandom is deep and personal. Tap into this by creating ways for them to connect with your characters or your author personality.

No matter where you fall on the spectrum of author-focused or story-world-focused branding, you must be consistent.

As we descend deeper into the layers, we will transition from social and group dynamics into personal behavior and psychology, discussing principles like fluency, availability and recency. You'll begin to see how these layers aren't distinct but interconnected. The work you do at the mesoscopic layer reinforces work at the microscopic layer and vice versa. I design all of this work to feedback to the macroscopic layer, where cumulative advantage manifests in the market.

A BRAND PROMISE KEPT

All good brands have a brand promise. The brand promise is what the user of the brand should expect from its use. Apple users trust the brand for simplicity, innovation, and creativity. In reality, Apple doesn't always have the most innovative product, but that doesn't change how their consumers feel about the overall brand. Those that join the cult of Apple know that they can trust the company to deliver over the long haul.

What is your brand promise?

Think through what readers will get from your books. It need not be unique, just consistent. If the system and fans are to do the heavy lifting, we need to give them proper tools. Make it easy for them to articulate that promise at an emotional level to win over other fans.

This is pattern matching. Some might see it as brainwashing. When asked, you want a fan to provide a congruent message to others. I'm not talking about going full *Manchurian Candidate*, where everyone repeats "Raymond Shaw is the kindest, bravest, most wonderful human being I've ever known in my life." Rather that you make it easy and available for a reader to understand the brand and the value it offers.

If you can define something unique, then it becomes easier to differentiate your brand from others in a similar genre. In the end, you want to be able to deliver when a fan recommends your book to others.

As an author, we focus on reviews as social proof. Having a written review is concrete validation of our work, but these aren't the reviews that will matter for building an enduring brand. What really matters are those reviews and recommendations made over drinks or after dinner between friends. The brand promise is there to back up when a fan says to a friend, "You really need to read this book because…" You are responsible for closing that loop when the friend picks up your book, by delivering on the brand promise voiced by your fan.

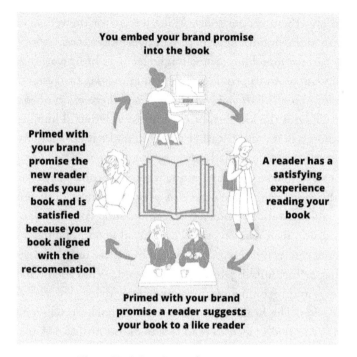

Figure 18: A Promise Made a Promise Kept

WELCOME TO YOUR BRAND FANTASY

You're a better marketer than you know. In *Brand Seduction*,[1] Daryl Weber explores using behavioral psychology to create a brand fantasy. His view is that brand fantasy is aligned with Demasio's Somatic Marker hypothesis, meaning that rather than seeking a literal expression of brand, you seek to create an emotional connection, something ephemeral that becomes part of the fan's psyche. This isn't an attempt to evoke emotion, rather to create an emotional bond and an experience that the reader seeks to fulfill by reading more of your books.

I believe this may be one of the most important ideas in marketing. Reflect on your own emotional association with a brand, let's say for your favorite book. Sure, there may be a quote or two you have memorized, but the real tie is how you feel when you recall the experience of reading the book. It's a story about the story. Your remembering self is retelling the tale of what you experienced when reading that book.

The areas of memory and emotion are driven by the fast-thinking, unconscious parts of the brain. These areas are willingly opened up by the reader when they read your book and imagine the story in their mind's eye. We will go deeper into this concept when we delve into the microscopic layer, where we will unlock how to embed the brand fantasy.

As a writer, you think of characters as a story device. Main and supporting characters will go through story arcs and react to conflict. You may use archetypes to design your characters, so they connect with a reader's psyche or trigger an emotion. Think about the brand fantasy in a similar way.

What takeaway emotions are you looking for a reader to have? What is the atmosphere of your story world, and do you reflect and connect to it in your marketing and communication?

Too often, authors resort to closing strategies in marketing and advertising. If you regularly get reviews where people are calling out characters they relate to, or character relationships that readers envy, then these are what you want to infuse into the brand.

DEFINING YOUR TRIBE

In *Primalbranding*,[2] Patrick Hanlon states that great brands have seven characteristics of a religion or tribe. Apple has been described as a cult, and so too have fans of sports teams. I don't see all of his seven characteristics as necessary, but I do ascribe to the idea that good brands create community and become part of our identity. By creating a creed, icons, rituals, identifying pagans and non-believers, and creating a sense of belonging, your brand takes on a social aspect that aligns with your community. You'll see in later chapters how having the common interest of your brand becomes a unifying component of your community.

Some authors look at readers only as consumers. There is some truth to this assumption, and there is a segment of your readers that only care about when the next book is out. Even if they've gone to the effort of signing up for your newsletter, all they care about is a notification of your next book release. If this is how you treat your readers, then why should you ever expect them to see your work as anything more than transactional?

Nor should you expect everyone that picks up one of your books will sign up for your emails or join the community. Fans need to be treated the way you like to be treated, and then a little better because they are the source of your income.

If your communications and community are all based on the sale of a book, don't be surprised that you're treated like a transaction. You don't want to be the hired help, and they don't want to be seen as your bank. To counter this, you need to build a brand aligned to community.

Let's discover what's behind a healthy community.

7
YOUR COMMUNITY

 "Why shouldn't truth be stranger than fiction? Fiction, after all, has to make sense."

— MARK TWAIN

YOUR SOCIAL BRAIN

It took millions of years for us to develop the brains we have today. In William Von Hippel's book, The Social Leap,[1] he shares how our ape-ish ancestors began coordinating behavior. At first, it was a means to survive. By forming a group, Australopithecus could fend off predators by staying together and hurling rocks. As we began operating in social structures, our brains adapted to deal with a more dangerous situation – our fellow homo sapiens.

Archeological evidence shows a rapid increase in skull volume as our species became social. We needed more and different brain capacity to navigate society. Emotions like pride, guilt, shame, envy all came out of our social situation. We needed these emotions for us deal with the dynamics of the group and to maintain social status and membership within our tribe.

Our lives depended on the tribe, and our mental health is still tied to our social interaction. We seek those like ourselves. Today, many do this through popular culture rather than politics or religion. We are hardwired for social interaction, and we can use this need for community to build cumulative advantage.

WHY DO YOU NEED A COMMUNITY?

The purpose of your community must be higher than just selling books, otherwise, there will be no reason for a community to form. The group's purpose should revolve around the story world experience, the delivery of a personal emotional experience, and the meeting of psychological needs. Beyond the purpose of the group as a whole, you must help members see their individual purpose within the group. We all strive for meaning in our lives. You foster belonging by giving people a means to feel needed and have meaning within the community. Would you be happy in a group if your purpose was just to buy stuff?

DON'T MISTAKE SOCIAL MEDIA FOR COMMUNITY OR PLATFORM.

Just like social media platforms can be mistaken for a social network, a community platform like Facebook Groups or Mighty Networks can be mistaken for community. These platforms are tools to facilitate a community, but without community dynamics, they will never flourish.

Being on social media does not mean you have a social network. Social media is a tool to disseminate and amplify your messaging. *What drives results is the connections and constituents of your network*. Too often, we look to the newest social media platform to be the panacea for a weak network. If your underlying network isn't designed right, then its messaging won't transmit, or it will spread to the wrong audience.

There is no need to envy influencers on Instagram or YouTubers that have created social media clout on their respective platforms. In 2018, Mention.com reported that only 2.1% of Instagram users had between 50,000 to 100,000 followers. Only 1.5% of Instagram users have over 500,000. There were only fifty-six mega-celebrities, with over ten million followers.[2]

A small group of winners with massive followings can create fortunes from their audience. Experts estimate the average annual revenue is $1,000 per 100,000 followers, and falls in a range of one to five cents a follower.[3]

Just like digital publishing, follower aggregation is driven by cumulative advantage with few winners, and many of those winners have leveraged previous celebrity to build an audience. How is it that followers are worth a penny each? Because it's not a community. If you're trying to build a big following on a social media platform, keep in mind that if it never becomes a community around your brand, it will be impossible to convert into revenue.

A Linqia survey of marketers using influencers as part of their media strategy showed that 52% of marketers see the most significant challenge as showing ROI for the investment in influencer media[4]. This is the dirty industry secret that will eventually stop money flowing to influencers. Don't copy that model; it is less profitable than publishing.

You may hear authors saying you need to build a platform to sell your books. Furthermore, that platform needs to be proprietary, so you have 100% control of how it is used. Building that platform on Facebook or Patreon leaves you vulnerable to their terms of service. While at face value, this is all excellent advice and likely comes from an author's experience and success, it doesn't provide the whole picture.

Readers don't seek platforms. They seek community. A platform is a tool just like other social media platforms. Better, because you own it, but lifeless if it doesn't have a community.

Duncan Wordle worked for Disney for twenty years and was in charge of innovation. I heard him speak about how they looked to increase revenues at the theme parks. Now, the finance guys would suggest just raising ticket prices. Sure, some folks would whine, and some wouldn't go, but I know from my pricing experience that the price increase would offset any loss in attendance.

That's not what Disney did.

Instead, they did an analysis of what guests didn't like about the parks, and the biggest was standing in lines. They provided RFID technology to guests willing to pay more, so they never stood in line. They could also improve the experience by using the RFID to be your room key, wallet, and dinner reservation check-in – the key to the Kingdom.

This enhanced the user experience and increased revenues. Not just because folks will pay a premium to not stand in line, but by saving the time they stood in lines, guests spent more money. His team understood that people are there for an experience, and the more time they can give them with friends and family having that experience, the more they spend money.

You see, the Magic Kingdom is a shopping mall in disguise as a community experience. They don't have to sell you because you want to buy.

Authors, it's time to abandon the sales funnel conversion model and construct a community that serves your audience. A reader desires an experience, not marketing. *Marketing pushes information at a subject. Experiences attract the prospect.* Create content that elicits emotional experiences, not calls to action.

We will build your customer nurturing engine on processes that:

- remind your readers of those experiences,
- create new emotions,
- fulfill social needs,
- provide them with ways to share and socialize those experiences.

Along the way, there will be times to buy, and they will do it willingly without being beaten over the head with deals and calls to action.

Jono Bacon, the author of *People Powered*,[5] has a system called SCARF. He managed tech communities like the UBUNTU user group and consults with companies on community-building. He thinks we should view the user community of a company as an asset and as a product. By having a community that delivers SCARF, you'll increase engagement and get users to contribute.

SCARF stands for:

Status: People seek status within the group. Social standing is an organizing principle. Some will seek to contribute more and expect status rewards.

Certainty: Avoid uncertainty. We look to have stability in our lives and reduce risk and uncertainty. Being part of a group can provide us with social certainty. By the same token, if joining the group is confusing, or the process is uncertain, then we risk triggering feelings of doubt that will cause defection from the community or poor onboarding.

Autonomy: People want to have control and independence, or at least feel that they have it. I'll share with you in later chapters how the readers of The Four Horsemen Universe have been given autonomy to run their own fan club. Part of autonomy is choice. By giving community members options for how they take part, you increase the freedom they feel they have.

Relatedness: We want to be part of something. This goes back to our tribal instincts and our need to associate with those like us. All communities are based on an associative principle and create homophily or commonality.

Fairness: We seek to be treated fairly. This isn't a call for equality; rather, when people feel the community isn't being fair, they will see it as a threat.

STOP GUMMING UP THE WORKS

Why go to all this trouble building a community when you're just trying to sell books?

We're not just trying to sell books. We are building a cumulative advantage engine that, once primed, sells more and more books each cycle. By the time you descend through this mesoscopic layer, you will understand why social media may dampen your ability to build cumulative advantage. Every post you send out in hopes of it going viral could damage your network. To set the stage, you must look at some research – old research, from before the advent of social media.

Let's travel back in time to 1964. Stanley Milgram, a famous social psychologist, is working at Harvard. He is best known for his obedience to authority experiments. Those experiments were controversial, and he has now moved on to a less contentious subject: social connections.

While he isn't the guy who came up with the idea that we are all connected by six degrees of separation, his experiment validated that idea. He showed the average number of links between any two people is 5.8, or what we commonly refer to as six degrees of separation. The experiment was called the 'Small World Problem,'[6] and they conducted it before the internet existed.

The experiment asked subjects in Nebraska to send a letter to a stockbroker in Boston. The rules were that they could only send the letter directly to the person if they knew them on a first-name basis. Otherwise, they were directed to send the letter to someone that they knew on a first-name basis that might know the stockbroker.

Stanley's research says you're only six connections from everyone that would want to read your book. Why is it that a professor with only the post office as a tool could make connections between a specific target and a bunch of random people, but even with today's technology, we aren't efficiently connecting to our desired audiences? Why isn't just asking friends and family to buy your book enough to start an information cascade and rocket you up the bestseller charts? Don't you know five friends and they know five friends, and so on, and so on?

THE OTHER VILLAINOUS FORCE: INERTIA

Diving deeper into Milgram's research, we see that getting started is more than half the problem. In the study, only twenty-one percent of the folders were delivered. Of those not delivered, fifty-four percent never made it to a second hand-off[7]. The chain died with either the first or second person passing the folder.

Just like Milgram's chain letter, your viral marketing dies in the hands of friends, fans, and family.

There was more to this experiment. Of the nearly three hundred subjects, one hundred were from Boston. Of the other two hundred from Nebraska, one hundred were all blue-chip stock investors. Only one hundred were from a random address list.

Why is this important? Only ninety-eight people in Nebraska were random subjects, and of those, only eighteen completed the chain with a mean chain length of 5.7. The other two groups tested the ideas of geographic similarity and subject similarity. The Boston group delivered twenty-two letters with a mean chain length of 4.4. The Nebraska Stockholders delivered twenty-four letters with a mean chain length of 5.4.

It is here that we can unravel why we struggle to connect with the right audience on social media, when the myth is that it could be done randomly by mail.

Milgram created groups with homophily, a type of commonality. One subgroup consisted of stock investors; the other was close in geography (same town as the target). Within common interest groups, subjects have stronger connections and improved common knowledge of like people.

Is there a good chance that you could make connections to a stranger in the same profession or hometown? Indeed, the probability is higher.

Another exciting development in the experiment was, of the sixty-four delivered letters, forty-eight percent went through three key connectors or shared channels. Milgram called these penultimate links. Key brokers of a social network. Today, these may be referred to as influencers.

Back in the 1960s, network analysis was in its early days. Now we have a language to talk about how networks work and ways to define network characteristics. Milgram was part of this foundational work to see how specific nodes act as a brokerage between strangers.

Now I'll share research focused directly on social networks and communication that reveals the friction and resistance inherent in the network. You can organize a different type of community, one that uses correct network design to overcome inertia and accumulate advantage.

Imagine structuring a community where, behind the scenes, users were compelled to share or grow the community. We will look into Dr. Centrolla's work on how behaviors are established in groups. He has been a thought leader on the topic of community behavior and network communication. His book *How behavior Spreads*[8] and his other research was eye-opening to me, and fundamental to my ideas on how you need a community that is designed to influence behavior. His research on social convention development, where subjects were rewarded when they came to an agreement on the name for a baby, and the "Emperor's Dilemma" experiment, where he evaluated the ability of a network to resist or spread a social norm supported by a few fanatics, shows that most viral marketing fails because of network suitability.

Simply put, trying to disseminate a complex behavior change via a system designed to transmit a simple message will fail. Specific network conditions need to be in place for complex behaviors to spread, and this is where most marketing falls apart. At their best, social media systems are massive weak-link systems that have the potential to broker your message across a network; at worst, they slow down behavior change because the network link is weak[9]. We will dive deeper into what is explicitly stopping your network from sharing, just like Milgram's subjects didn't pass on those folders.

Milgram's attempt to send a message across the country shows, on the one hand, the ease of a message getting to the right source, and on the other, the inherent problems with getting your network to do your bidding. One would think, with the technology advances since Milgram's small-world experiment, that messages would spread faster than ever before. In some cases, they do. In the Milgram study, the obstacle wasn't the number of links in the chain. Instead, it was how often the chain broke. It was a complex task requiring someone to think through the problem, then mail the letter on to the best solution they had. In the twenty-first century, it's easier to click or email then send something by mail, so why doesn't your message go viral, or at least get to the right audience?

There are two reasons your messages don't spread. The first is inertia. It's hard to get people to do things they don't have an interest in doing. Secondly, social media is inherently flawed for what we are trying to do with it. To understand what's broken, why don't we begin with the holy grail of promotion – word of mouth. This is our endgame, after all, to have your fans bring up your books over drinks when asked what they've read recently.

The most powerful form of advertisement is word of mouth. In a 1987 study, Brown and Reingen tested how word-of-mouth referrals and recommendations worked in networks with strong and weak ties. Tie strength was part of Granovetter's 1973 research,[10] where he showed that weak ties could spread messages better across social networks.

A weak tie is those relationships you have with acquaintances versus the strong ties of deeper relationships. Granovetter's seminal work is often cited as the reason that social networks are so powerful. The Brown and Reingen study wanted to test word of mouth and how it related to the types of ties people have with each other.

Granovetter had already proved that weak ties are more likely than strong ties to serve as bridges between clusters, and could jump significant geographic and demographic distances. Weak ties can act like superhighways to get a message to move further and faster. When a consumer has social relations with both strong and weak ties that can be potential sources of referral, strong ties are more likely than weak ties to be activated. In the study, 27% (74 of 273) of the potential strong-tie sources were activated, as compared to 7% of weak ties for the referral flow.[11]

While weak ties have their place, data shows that when we are looking for recommendations, more often than not, we ask our strong ties – those we know and with whom we share common traits. "The more homophilous the tie, the more likely it would be activated from the set of potential sources of information. Of the activated ties, 37% were homophilous, compared to 22% of the nonactivated ties."[12]

In 2004, Wu and Huberman created a model to test how opinion formation spreads within social structures. In the computer simulations, people were of three opinions: yes, no, or undecided. The social network model randomized these opinions across members and tested various thresholds of opinion change. The researchers ran thousands of iterations. The research concluded that, given an arbitrary starting point, that the population holding a particular opinion didn't vary much from the original state.

The theory assumes asynchronous choices by individuals among two or three opinions, and it predicts the time evolution of the set of opinions from any arbitrary initial condition. We showed that under very general conditions, a martingale property ensues, i.e., the expected weighted fraction of the population that holds an

> *opinion is constant in time. By weighted fraction, we mean the fraction of individuals holding a given opinion, averaged over their social connectivity. Most importantly, this weighted fraction is not either zero or one, but corresponds to a non-trivial distribution in the long time limit. This coexistence of opinions within a social network is in agreement with the often observed locality effect, in which an opinion or a fad is localized to given groups without infecting the whole society.*[13]

Simply put, opinions don't change that much, even when millions of iterations are simulated. While opinions shift, they never entirely move to one or another option. These findings cast doubt on the applicability of tipping models to a number of consumer behaviors.[14] Is there no tipping point that will trigger cumulative advantage?

You now have seen research that shows that strong ties are respected more when word-of-mouth recommendations are given, and even more so if they are from people we deem are like us. The Hu opinion model suggests that a viral opinion change is difficult to reproduce even in mathematical models, and that in these experiments, people rarely shift from their original opinion. So how are you ever going to get people to join you in building cumulative advantage?

Centolla writes in *How Behavior Spreads*,

> *"Valuable information, for instance, about changing weather conditions or new media events, spreads quickly from person to person, as does more banal information about the score of a sporting event. If I learn the score of today's playoff game, I can easily repeat it at a party. Anyone who hears me also learns the score and can just as easily spread this information to others. No one needs to be coerced or pressured to adopt the informational contagion or to spread it. News propagates effortlessly through a network. For this reason, diseases and information are typically simple contagions, which only require a single activated contact for transmission.*
>
> *By contrast, social movements, complex information (such as urban legends, or rumors that require confirmation), social norms,*

medical and health-related behaviors, innovation adoption, and significant capital investments are different. They typically involve some kind of cost (financial, psychological, or reputational), risk, or complementarity, which increases an adopter's dependence on other people's decisions. The costlier, higher-risk or less familiar a behavior is, the more that the decision to adopt depends upon social confirmation."

Centolla's research argues that any meaningful behavior change, like buying a book or becoming a fan, is likely to be a complex contagion – that is, one requiring contact with multiple sources of reinforcement to be transmitted. For a complex contagion, a person's "threshold" for adoption is higher than one interaction and is defined as the number of activated contacts required to trigger her activation.

"Because the focal individual initially resists adopting a costly new behavior, she requires several of her contacts to adopt it before she will. Her threshold for activation can only be overcome if she receives sufficient social reinforcement from her network to encourage her to adopt. Thus, while multiple exposures to the same infected individual may be sufficient for simple contagions to spread, multiple sources of exposure are needed to diffuse complex contagions."[15]

Centolla shares there are at least four social mechanisms that explain why it requires multiple exposures to adopt a complex behavior.

Strategic complementarity: The value of a behavior increases with the number of others who adopt it.
Credibility: The more people who adopt a behavior, the more believable it is that the behavior is beneficial, or that it is worth the cost of adoption.
Legitimacy: The more people who adopt a behavior, the greater the expectation is that other people will approve of the decision to adopt, and the lower the risk of embarrassment or sanction.

Emotional contagion: The excitement associated with adopting a behavior increases with the number of others who embrace it.[16]

The result you seek isn't virality; it's cumulative advantage. Cumulative advantage is the indirect result of complex personal and social behavior. The behavior has risks, more than just sending Milgram's letter or commenting on your post. At a minimum, you are asking someone to risk both money for a book and the time to read it.

The secret is to build a network that promotes a complex contagion and rewards those who take part.

Rather than let an arbitrary network build and call it a community, you can build the *right* network and call it *your* community.

The essence of Centolla's work is the discovery of the *unsuitability of a typical network*. Few people set out to deliberately design a social network. If you're an author, the usual tools for building a fan base have more to do with selling than a social connection. This creates a more extensive network faster, but with weak ties or no ties between members.

Weak ties work well for spreading messages and can connect smaller clusters with a common tie but lack the influence to trigger complex behavior. Strong ties, particularly in densely clustered networks, have the structure to trigger complex behavior change through imitation, peer pressure, and emotional contagion, but are slow to diffuse information.

In a computer simulation where it was required for two neighbors to adopt before a node would also adopt the behavior, Centolla showed that a dense network with strong ties took twenty-six days to diffuse to all members fully. When three weak ties were introduced, the time to saturation went to thirty-five days. When the simulation doubled the number of weak ties after day one hundred, the diffusion had essentially stopped. Therefore, the very structure of most social network platforms kills a complex contagion rather than spreads it.[17]

The problem is, with a simple diffusion, the bridge from one network to another is typically one edge (connection), but if you need multiple adoptions by neighbors, then the bridge from cluster to cluster needs to be far denser. The density of links needs to be equal to the threshold value that causes a trigger.

In computer simulations of networks, mathematical formulas can be set for a threshold value before a simulation plays out. Not so easy in the real world where what causes a threshold trigger is more nebulous. Here in the real world of selling books, where we don't have a formula, we will need to overcompensate and build redundancy in our network so that a participant's threshold will be triggered.

The analogy of a forest fire can serve us to understand what is required for your marketing.

Forests need to have certain conditions in place for there to be a wildfire. There needs to be a density of trees and underbrush, dry conditions, and finally, a source of ignition. Not every lightning strike starts a wildfire; sometimes it burns a small area around the tree it hit and creates a natural firebreak. Another strike in that location will be met with conditions unsuitable for a conflagration.

Conditions for a wildfire build over time as underbrush density increases. We will focus on just that: creating the conditions that make complex contagion spread more suitable.

Imagine a hypothetical forest laid out on a checkerboard. In each square, there is a slot for a tree. If there is a tree, then no other tree can grow there. Each year, there is a probability of a tree growing in the slot by seeding from existing trees. There is a probability of a tree growing in an adjacent square from where a tree exists, and a probability of a tree growing two squares away that is half the probability of the adjoining square.

If a fire starts in a square, it will spread to adjacent squares where there is a tree. Empty squares are fire breaks that stop the fire from passing to further trees.

Each year, there is a lightning season, during which it is dry in our imaginary forest, and there is a one percent chance that lightning will strike a square. Over time, even though the possibility of a strike hasn't changed – it is still one percent for each square – once per season, the probability of a wildfire occurring will increase. The underlying cause being the increased number of trees from the seed propagation rule.

Now, imagine in this hypothetical model, we introduce a new type of tree, one whose probability to seed adjacent squares is double that of existing trees. Even if the probability remains the same for two squares out, just by doubling the adjacent square propagation, it will only be a matter of rounds before our new tree becomes the dominant tree in our forest – that is cumulative advantage in action.

The more time between lightning strikes, the denser the forest will become and the higher the probability of building the conflagration on the next strike.

We set out to get the forest thick with trees – your trees. Let others focus on the lightning strike while you quietly create the conditions for a wildfire. If you find yourself wondering how many times you need to post to keep an audience engaged, you're trying to make lightning, not build a forest. Focus on trying to get more trees planted in denser clumps. Propagate the conditions that result in homogeneity, particularly a commonality around your brand experience.

THE MESO-NEURO FEEDBACK LOOP AND HOW TO CREATE CUMULATIVE ADVANTAGE.

As we go deeper, you will see recurring themes. At the very core of everything we discuss is a reader and meeting their social and personal needs. Sometimes these needs are met internally via the reader's pursuit of meaning in their life, or desire to self-actualize. In other instances, we can only reach the need through engagement with others. A brand promise to help fulfill some of these needs will compel readers to the brand. Then, fulfilling these needs through your story and your community will turn your brand fantasy into your reader's new religion.

The redundancy and reinforcement at the mesoscopic and neuroscopic levels isn't an accident. We're fighting inertia and looking to create new pattern-matching that results in complex behavior adoption. When you come up from the depths of the neuroscopic level and build your cumulative advantage system, having these redundancies and positive feedback loops to reinforce behavior will expedite the accumulation of fans – planting more trees. This is the self-organizing function of your system.

We're not done talking about building your community. We will explore community-building activities later. Before doing that work, we need to descend deeper, going down another layer to the neuroscopic level – inside the reader's mind.

Reader by reader, you create a community. It will be in the reading process that you get individuals to associate their identity with your brand, and feel they need to belong to your community. To accomplish this, you will need to understand the inner workings of the human mind and unleash your secret weapon to win over readers.

If being a best-selling author is your goal, then it's time to get inside the head of a reader and learn how to hack their wetware.

THE MICROSCOPIC LAYER

aka the Neuroscopic Layer
Where the Connection to the Individual Is Made

8
IT'S ALL IN YOUR HEAD

> *"Reason is the natural order of truth; but imagination is the organ of meaning."*
>
> — C.S. LEWIS

Accordion to scientists, most people will not notice that the first word in this sentence was a musical instrument. If you missed the word and unconsciously substituted *according*, does that mean you're a lazy reader? Quite the opposite; that is your brain quickly compensating and filling in the details it expects to see. Your brain is pattern matching.

In this chapter, we will explore what happens inside the brain of a reader. The building block of all cumulative advantage for an author is the reader. If you are some other content producer, then it's the ultimate consumer of that content.

An author's wealth is derived from readers seeing the value in their storytelling, and that value exceeding the money requested for the story. If you are to retain that reader, then a critical value proposition needs to be met: the emotional payoff must outweigh the time and brainpower to consume that story. Keep in mind getting a reader to use their brain has a real caloric cost. The brain is our most energy intensive organ, and we are designed to conserve calories.

While cumulative advantage is a macro force, to harness it, we are going to focus on the other end of the spectrum on what I call the microscopic layer. Sometimes I refer to it as the neuroscopic layer, because where the magic happens is within a reader's neurons. We need to get inside the brain of your reader and use the access you're given to establish an emotional connection. If cumulative advantage is built by getting a reader to undertake a series of complex and risky behaviors, then we need to influence those behaviors.

The behaviors and their associated risks are:

1. Buy your book – financial risk.
2. Read your book – time risk.
3. Read more of your works – added financial and time risk.
4. Establish an emotional connection and identity association – time risk.
5. Establish a social relationship – time and social risk.
6. Advocate to others – reputational risk.

The first step may be satisfied by using marketing funnels and conversion strategies; however, we can achieve none of the other steps with sales tactics. This is why most authors fail at building an audience.

The irony is that you've had the secret to success the whole time. Read on to get a deeper understanding of this secret influence that you have over readers.

In his book *Thinking, Fast and Slow*,[1] Kahneman describes two systems of thinking. System one, our ancient lizard brain, is designed to react quickly to the environment and keep us safe. Our slower system, system two, is our rational thinking, which we use for complex tasks. What Kahneman proposes is that our logical reasoning (system two) is heavily influenced by the unconscious system one. While we think we are rational and calculated in our decision-making, it is clouded by those unconscious mental shortcuts and our memories.

Let's go deeper into the unconscious, then explore memory and emotion. If you understand these concepts, you'll understand how authors have a secret passage into a reader's unconscious mind where they can embed deep learning and an emotional connection.

Looking at the picture of the two tables, pick the table that is longer.

Figure 19: Table Illusion

Now measure the length and width of both tables. You'll confirm that the tables are identical in length and width.

Even with this information and the application of your rational thinking, your brain keeps interpreting the left table as longer and thinner. Along with that illusion, your brain is doing millions of other alterations to keep the image sharp and make it easier for you to interpret.

What you perceive can be influenced. Look below and read down, then across.

Figure 20: Letter Number Illusion

We see the middle either as a B or a thirteen, depending on whether we're reading down or across.

You may have seen other optical illusions throughout your life, and even after having them explained, they still play tricks on the eye. The reality is that we are heavily influenced by the context of the data we take in. Our brain is using that information and putting it in order for us to act upon it. Your reality isn't real; it is a perception of reality that your unconscious brain filters first before your conscious mind gets a chance to have its say about this perception.

Tversky and Kahneman (1974) showed that our decision-making is heavily influenced by biases and mental shortcuts (heuristics). Behavioral economists have identified and named hundreds of heuristics and biases used to navigate our environment. These mental shortcuts occur unconsciously and influence our choices. Here are some examples;

- **Familiarity Heuristic:** A mental shortcut applied to various situations in which individuals assume that the circumstances underlying the past behavior still hold true for the present situation, and that the past behavior thus can be correctly applied to the new situation.
- **Bandwagon Effect:** The tendency to do (or believe) things because many other people do (or believe) the same.

- **Confirmation Bias:** The tendency to search for, interpret, focus on, and remember information in a way that confirms one's perceptions.

These are but a few of the biases and heuristics we use to navigate our surroundings and social situations. We build these rules on pattern matching. To deal with the billions of sensory inputs we are subjected to on a minute by minute basis, our lizard brain uses pattern matching to protect us.

Any stimulus activates our brain. The brain filters much of the stimuli out, never allowing it to surface in our consciousness. System one uses the power of fast pattern matching to assess our environment and trigger fight-or-flight responses, then these patterns become physical patterns in our grey matter. Neuron bundles and synapse connections between different areas of brain function are then triggered and ingrain the pattern.

Existing brain patterns are potent influences, as they trigger an emotional and physical response. Only then do we apply rationality and meaning to the experience. Recent research by Libet and others validates that much of our rational decisions originate in our unconscious.[2]

What if even your conscious choices could be predicted by observing your brain waves? This isn't some crazy science fiction plot, but the research of Benjamin Libet. Libet measured electrical potential in specific locations of the brain before the act of deciding something. He called this 'readiness potential'.[3] The readiness potential typically occurred 350 milliseconds before the action.

Haynes confirmed these results and took the research further, showing via functional MRI what sections of the brain pre-charged before a willing act. The results could predict the subject's choice as many as ten seconds before they made it.[4]

This isn't to say you don't have free will; you just need to understand that a lot is going on in your head before you become aware, and the unconscious activity influences your decisions. System two rationalizes and applies meaning to behavior rather than initiates the behavior.

The rationalization of unconscious action has been scientifically validated in research with patients that suffer from lesions between the right and left-brain hemispheres. Gazzaniga showed in studies of patients where the left and right side of the brain has been split that the patient's brain made unconscious associations and then rationalized the decision.

Dr. Gazzaniga shared in the study,

"A number of years ago, we observed how the left dominant speaking hemisphere dealt with the behaviors we knew we had elicited from the disconnected right hemisphere. We first revealed the phenomenon using a simultaneous concept test. The patient is shown two pictures, one exclusively to the left hemisphere and one exclusively to the right, and is asked to choose from an array of pictures placed in full view in front of him the ones associated with the pictures lateralized to the left and right brain. In one example of this kind of test, a picture of a chicken claw was flashed to the left hemisphere, and a picture of a snow scene to the right hemisphere. Of the array of pictures placed in front of the subject, the obviously correct association is a chicken for the chicken claw and a shovel for the snow scene. Case PS responded by choosing the shovel with the left hand and the chicken with the right. When asked why he chose these items, his left hemisphere replied, "Oh, that's simple. The chicken claw goes with the chicken, and you need a shovel to clean out the chicken shed." Here, the left brain, observing the left hand's response, interprets that response into a context consistent with its sphere of knowledge, one that does not include information about the left hemisphere snow scene. We called this left hemisphere process the 'interpreter.'"[5]

This rationalization of choice observed by Dr. Gazzaniga in patients with split brains is present in us all and essential to influencing behavior. Rather than appealing to the rational mind to make a sale with logic, you can activate a pattern that triggers emotion in the unconscious. If the behavior creates a satisfying feeling, the reader will repeat the behavior and use their rational mind to give the pattern meaning. In essence, they will sell themselves.

Gazzaniga also penned the book *The Consciousness Instinct: Unraveling the Mystery of How the Brain Makes the Mind*.[6] The premise of the book is that our mind results from a myriad of systems in our brain working together. He posits that consciousness is an advanced instinct that has bubbled up from the interaction of various subsystems of the brain, and doesn't exist in any one single spot.

After observing patients with all types of damage to distinct parts of the brain, he concluded that consciousness appears to be very resilient in the sense that it remains intact. The issue is that damage to the underlying unconscious brain influences our consciousness, but the patients with the impairment are unaware of this influence.

Antonio Damasio's Somatic Marker Hypothesis also comes from researching patients with brain lesions. Damasio conducted a famous experiment called "the Iowa Gambling Task".[7] Subjects were presented with decks of cards and asked to gamble money. They were given a combination of good and bad decks, and after forty to fifty tries with a deck, most subjects could detect which was which. Subjects with damage to the orbitofrontal cortex could not differentiate good from bad decks and continued to lose at the gambling task.

The experiment was also able to measure skin conductivity, "sweaty palms," in subjects in anticipation of bad decks. The experiment showed that there is a physical-emotional component in our decision-making process. Damasio hypothesizes that our process is influenced by emotional reactions that have a strong somatic (bodily) response.

If this is true, then emotional influence is critical to our reader's decision as to the value of a book.

"So, all I need to do is charge up the emotion in my books?"

Not quite.

The misconception is if you get your readers to feel the emotion, they will be hooked. This isn't exactly right. We all have experienced commercials that pull on our heartstrings, but they don't get us to be invested in the brand. While you need to have your readers move through an emotional spectrum to deliver a satisfying story, there needs to be a definite feeling of satisfaction with the overall product and brand experience.

Have you ever gone back to watch an old movie or read a book and found it wasn't what you remembered? The problem wasn't that you forgot the story; instead, there was a disconnect in your memory of how exceptional it was, and when re-watching, you don't get that same emotional charge.

For me, it was *Escape from New York*. I was fifteen when the movie came out. The special effects were top-notch, the dystopian ideas were timely, and the action was thrilling. Decades later, I re-watched the film, but a gap had developed between what I was currently experiencing and how I remembered the movie. I had seen it several times, so it wasn't a matter of not recalling the plot progression – instead, it was a disconnect between my memory and my experience of the material. What I saw now conflicted with my recollection and how I felt about the movie.

I had a similar experience years ago when I had my first visit to Disney World as an adult. My adult experience of "It's a Small World" left me disappointed and disjointed. The later experience conflicted with the memory of happiness and satisfaction.

This is Kahneman's experiencing self and remembering self in action, and it has a lot to do with happiness and satisfaction. Kahneman contends that our remembering self drives a large part of our decision-making.

He uses the example of people's recollection of medical procedures. Patients were asked to rate the pain during the procedure (this is your experiencing self). Later, the patients were asked to rate the pain of the procedure recalling and interpreting the data (the remembering self). Patients that had more pain at the end of the procedure described the procedure as more painful in recollection than those who had less pain at the end.

We become an ***unconscious storyteller*** to ourselves, reconstructing past events with our cognitive spin. What if you as the author could influence how readers remember your content? We want our readers to feel satisfied with our content, but how do you do this?

Emotion is an interesting phenomenon. Paul Ekman's work shows six emotions are universally recognized.[8] People can identify these emotions just by facial expressions, regardless of if those people speak the same language. These emotions are happiness, sadness, fear, disgust, anger, and surprise, and they are reactions triggered by our interaction with the environment.

I believe that all authors want the reader to feel satisfaction, rather than one of the six recognizable emotions, when finished reading a book. *"But I write horror, don't I want the reader to feel fear while reading?"* Yes, but you must differentiate the emotional journey or arc you send your readers on versus how they assess the overall experience of your product.

We want them to feel contentment about the choice of investing in you as an author. We are establishing a pattern between the activator of buying and reading your book, and triggering the feeling of satisfaction. Closing the loop between the payoff of satisfaction from the risk they took in buying the book and investing the time to read it. Satisfaction is the story we tell ourselves after the experience, with Kahneman's remembering self.

I believe that satisfaction and happiness have a lot to do with Maslow's hierarchy of human needs, or Joe Griffen and Ivan Tyrell's human givens[9]. Maslow and Griffen describe systems focused on getting a range of human needs met for a happy and healthy life. When we don't have these needs met, it creates at a *minimum* dissatisfaction, and can escalate into fear, longing, anger, frustration, and, at its worst, mental illness.

Maslow postulated that all humans require love and belonging (friendship, intimacy, family, sense of connection) and esteem (respect, self-esteem, status, recognition, strength, and freedom). While Maslow points the direction, I suggest applying the concepts from the Human Givens Approach[10] developed by Joe Griffen and Ivan Tyrell.

If you can address these needs at the unconscious level with your community and with your books, then the reader will connect your books as the activator for happiness and satisfaction.

Griffen and Tyrell suggest nine basic human givens for mental health and well-being:

1. **Security**: A sense of safety and security; safe territory; an environment in which we can live without experiencing excessive fear so that we can develop healthily.

2. **Autonomy and control**: A sense of independence and control over what happens around and to us.
3. **Status**: A sense of status – being accepted and valued in the various social groups we belong to.
4. **Privacy**: Time and space enough to reflect on and consolidate our experiences.
5. **Attention**: Receiving attention from others, but also giving it; a form of the essential nutrition that fuels the development of each individual, family, and culture.
6. **Connection to the wider community**: Interaction with a larger group of people and a sense of being part of the group.
7. **Intimacy**: Emotional connection to other people – friendship, love, affection, fun.
8. **Competence and achievement**: A sense of our own ability and achievements; that we have what it takes to meet life's demands.
9. **Meaning and purpose**: Being stretched, aiming for meaningful goals, having a sense of a higher calling, or serving others creates meaning and purpose.

I have cross-referenced these with Maslow's hierarchy to come up with the following brief list:

- Security and Safety
- Belonging, connection with a broader community
- Status, esteem,
- Intimacy
- Attention
- Autonomy and control
- Purpose/ Self Actualization

The human givens hypothesis aligns Gazzaniga's and Kahneman's work that much of our behavior manifests in unconscious areas of our brain, creating physical and emotional responses (system one thinking).

It's no surprise that some of these align with Bacon's SCARF model (Status, Certainty, Autonomy, Relatedness, Fairness). We tie much of our mental health to socialization. As you implement your system, you will see how community mirrors and validates the individual's feelings and reinforces the patterns established in your books.

What if we could establish a pattern where the use of your products and participation in your community satisfied the human givens?

Can we use Kahneman's remembering self to interpret the experience and change behavior?

While basic instincts and emotions drive our behavior and immediate response, we also have higher functions like memory, imagination, a rational mind, metaphorical understanding, and the ability to observe ourselves.[11] Memory allows us to learn from our past. A metaphorical mind and imagination enable us to draw from abstract concepts and contemplate "what if" situations. Our rational mind, along with the ability to get outside of our thoughts, is a way to apply meta-learning from our actions.

How memory and imagination work are still far more mystery than science. The purpose of this book isn't to understand their workings but to harness their power. If you were to close your eyes and imagine a purple elephant, a picture of a purple elephant wouldn't appear inside your eyelids. Even with concentration, you would be hard-pressed to create visual representations, nor would the words PURPLE or ELEPHANT, or a definition of either scroll across your mind's eye. Instead, when you are imagining, you activate memory and associations from past experiences to understand the concept.

Memory is associative, creating relationships between our senses, thoughts, and interpretations of experience. But semantics play a dominant role in our experience of the world. Neuro-linguists would argue that language is the most influential framework, as it is linked to how we communicate our ideas to others, as well as categorize and recall memory and concepts.

Back to our purple elephant, the purple elephant isn't a picture or a word; it's you activating associations from past experiences to understand the concept.

Recalling a memory is a physical process. fMRI can capture

activation in our brains. In a 2009 study, scientists could use fMRI scans and a computer algorithm to literally read a person's mind.[12] With machine learning, a computer was able to roughly recreate visual patterns like letters and symbols through interpreting brain activity.

HERE LIES THE POWER OF A STORYTELLER.

Through words and the reader's imagination, you are given access to the reader's mind. They give you permission to the brain centers that drive imagination, emotion, and memory. Your story, in most respects, is indiscernible in the brain from reality. It triggers neurons to fire, and establishes neural pathways, just like an actual experience. The difference is that through our rational mind, we can differentiate between real and imaginary.

The human givens approach is built on the concept that patterns drive much of our life. Through pattern matching, an activator triggers an emotion or instinct, and we respond with a behavior. It is after the fact that we rationalize the behavior. In this system, humans are driven toward achieving the "human givens," and patterns develop that either satisfy or substitute meeting these needs. Below, you can see the cognitive functions that Griffen and Tyrell suggest are the operating system for navigating the world and society.

- **Memory**: The ability to develop complex long-term memory, which enables people to add to their innate (instinctive) knowledge and learn.
- **Rapport**: The ability to build rapport, empathize, and connect with others.
- **Imagination**: Enables people to focus attention away from their emotions and problem-solve more creatively and objectively (a 'reality simulator').
- **Instincts and emotions**: A set of basic responses and 'propulsion' for behaviors.
- **A rational mind**: Conscious thought that can check out emotions, question, analyze, and plan.
- **A metaphorical mind**: The ability to 'know,' to understand

the world unconsciously through metaphorical pattern matching ('this thing is *like* that thing').
- **An observing self**: That part of us which can step back, be more objective, and recognize itself as a unique center of awareness apart from intellect, emotion, and conditioning.
- **A dreaming brain**: Metaphorically defusing emotionally arousing expectations not acted out during the previous day.[13]

As an author, your work comes to life for the reader at the intersection of imagination, memory, emotion, and metaphor. The reader recreates the story, characters, and world you imagine, but it is not an exact copy. Instead, it is manifested in their mind's eye with all of their biases, memories, and experiences, immediately embedding personalization. It is here where you can imprint patterns personalized to each reader.

If you satisfy unmet desires or meet the human need for inclusion and emotional connection, then your readers will assign personal meaning to your work.

We can use this open invite into a reader's mind – and specifically into the unconscious mind – to provide a feeling of satisfaction and happiness through meeting the human givens.

Let's not forget this book is about building cumulative advantage. We are looking to market products to a mass audience, and at this point, we are deep in the weeds; at the deepest layer, what I refer to as the neuroscopic layer, deep in the brain of an individual reader. We are looking at what you can do to make a reader's experience with your product so meaningful and personal that they want those they like and love to have the same experience. Most importantly, we want them to sell themselves.

Let me show you the key and how to use it.

9

YOUR SECRET WEAPON

 "There are no facts, only interpretations."

— *FRIEDRICH NIETZSCHE*

Have you ever been hypnotized or watched a stage hypnotist? I observed one at a Bar Mitzvah. This is the true test of hypnotism, as the hypnotist needs to deal with a bunch of energetic thirteen-year-olds, half of whom think they are smart enough to "fake out" the hypnotist. At this show, one of my sons, along with a half dozen of the other boys, became entranced and followed the suggestions.

Now you may be skeptical, and if you're a skeptic, I suggest you look at the research by Oakley and Halligan. They used an fMRI to measure pain centers in the brain and track activity for both real and hypnotically induced pain. fMRI scans showed similar areas and intensities of activation between the two. Even if you don't think a hypnotic suggestion is real, the person who has been induced with a suggestion does.[1]

So, what does this have to do with authors and marketing? Am I suggesting you hire a hypnotist to go to conventions and mesmerize prospective readers?

There is no need to, as a reader willingly enters into a hypnotic trance every time they open a book.

> *"We define a trance state, as do many others, as a focused state of attention during which wider environmental stimuli are ignored."*[2]

A hypnotic trance is nothing more than a state characterized by an absence of response to external stimuli and intense focus. Doesn't that sound like a fully immersed reader? The reality is that we spend most of our time in some state of trance. Have you ever driven home focused on a phone call or in your head about something, and then realize you got all the way home without really paying attention to the road? That was a trance state. And readers want to be in that "zone" while they read.

This is where authors have an advantage no other marketer has. While it is your story, the visualization and associations are the reader's creation. Your work will hardwire into the reader's brain at the synaptic level. Axions and dendrites will exchange neurotransmitters as the experiencing self reads your story and creates memories and emotions. The remembering self will recall the experience and use logic to rationalize future buying decisions and advocate your work to others.

You can build positive associations in a reader's 'system one,' associations with your characters, story world, brand, or author persona, the latter being more difficult. You do this by creating deep, personalized, positive emotions and memories aligned with the human givens. You provide the plans to the house, and the reader will build it. If the work is done right, you won't have to tell them what to say about your book; like the brain-damaged patient, they will rationalize their advocacy of your story because they feel so strongly about what they experienced. They will willingly shill your product via word of mouth.

The premise of this book is to build up from the realm of the unconscious rather than the rational. The lizard brain and social needs of the reader will do your heavy lifting if we get to engage those areas of the brain, not in a scammy way, but by satisfying the unconscious needs of the reader through a positive experience in their imagination. When your books and fan community fulfill the human givens in a way no real person or group can, then cumulative advantage builds effortlessly. Your fans will willingly advocate your books, not because you begged them, but because they need to evangelize to those they love about your brand. They will bring them in to the community you've built to share the experience.

For a content creator, your stories are your product, but story has been a powerful tool for communication and teaching since the dawn of man. Before the written word, stories were told from memory, and they will continue to exist and be told in new ways. The reason story resonates so deeply on an individual level is that all of us are storytellers. We tell each other stories when we share how our day went; we add color and meaning. Story is a way to connect and share the experience. We use stories to teach our children skills and morals. We even tell ourselves stories via the way our remembering selves interpret the memories from our experiencing selves.

Donald Miller is the author of *Building a Story Brand*,[3] a best-selling marketing book. The story brand concept is something his company has used to help customers break out of old marketing methods and tell their story. He has helped thousands of businesses change how they communicate with customers. The premise is to design your marketing around the Hero's Journey.

As an author, you're likely familiar with Joseph Campbell's hero's journey story structure. Countless craft books reference the architecture, and there are thousands of stories based on the model. Where Miller shakes things up is by instructing clients to tell a story where the customer is the hero, the company is the mentor, and their product is the magic to defeat the problem.

Milton Erickson, a psychiatrist and psychologist who used hypnotism as his primary therapy, often told stories. These stories were vital to his treatments, as they used metaphors to seed the patient with ideas. Here again, we see how story can be to our unconscious understanding. The beauty is that unlike Erickson, you won't have to induce patients. You have readers who are practiced at inducing themselves into a trance; all they need is a good book.

You're already good at the craft of story. Marketers would love to have the ability you have for creating an emotional connection with a prospect. Your product is a story, a Trojan horse that the reader willingly allows into their subconscious.

The irony is that rather than build from these strengths, we grasp on to marketing tools we aren't as comfortable with. Why? Because we have seen them work for others, and look to replicate those results. But content, especially fiction, is a unique product that allows us special privileges and opportunities.

In the chapter "Is There a Formula for Recognition and Popularity," I shared with you how one company has specialized in creating brands around dead people, turning these persons into iconic figures through story. While they were actual people, the persona we associate with their name has always been a story, and the value today is how that story is spun.

Today, Steve McQueen is being crafted as the King of Cool. When he was alive, he wasn't a fashion designer, yet with a well-crafted story, his character becomes a fashion icon. Why can't you do the same with your characters?

BLURRING THE LINES

I have a powerful imagination. As a boy, I spent countless hours in my head, daydreaming. Books, comics, and movies I had seen inspired much of my imaginary exploits. It was exciting to be able to go to places like Disney World or a renaissance faire, where I could be immersed in a reality similar to what I had imagined.

As time passed and I started my own family, I reached back into my childhood to share some of those stories. This created deeper connections because I revisited these old worlds and got to experience them with my children. New connections were made that included me experiencing the tales through my children's eyes.

Disney has known this for years. The idea of movies coming 'out of the vault' (this was before constant on-demand entertainment) was that every seven years, a new generation of humans was coming of age. Their parents would bring them to see these old films because they wanted to give their child the enjoyment they'd had, and vicariously relive the joy of childhood.

Why have Tolkien and Rowling been able to continue to be best-selling authors without a recent book? Simple: their stories have such a hold on fans, they indoctrinate their offspring.

Disney is well beyond this strategy now. Watch Duncan Wardle talk about how they think about experience in the parks. It is the driving principle of design.[4] They are experts at blurring the line between a story world and reality.

How you should merge reality and your stories will be up to you; only your imagination is the limiting factor. Creating a way for your readers to slip in and out of your content and pulling your imaginary world into their actual world is your unique selling proposition.

Your fictional characters can have the same power as Steve McQueen's ghost. While his spirit is being used to sell eyewear, your characters can strengthen their bonds with your readers to sell more books.

At this point, you may be at a loss for how to do this. You may even feel that your characters and story world can't be a powerful brand. That's okay, the next section of this book is dedicated to helping you think through application.

The point is that, as an author, you have a unique skill set and product with a story. Readers allow your product into their unconscious, and it is there that advertisers desire access. You routinely waltz around in your reader's unconscious, oblivious to how you've accessed the most precious intimate space.

Emotion and memory are closely tied to each other and the limbic system, a core component of system one thinking. There are multiple theories of emotion and how the mind and body react to an event. While there may be contention about the origin of emotion (if what we "feel" starts in the body or the brain), this isn't as important as understanding that emotion and memory are linked, and the links are powerful and physical.

Have you ever had the experience of encountering a smell, and it immediately causes you to recollect distant memories? When our system one is triggered, it engages those associations – a combination of emotion, memory, and physical reaction – to influence the present.

Work by Damasio on the somatic marker hypothesis suggests that emotion is a complex mix of brain activity, hormones, and physical reaction that results in a physiological response that can drive behavior.[5]

Let's drive some behavior!

UP FROM THE DEPTHS

10
USING THE KEY

 "If the truth contradicts deeply held beliefs, that is too bad."

— HANS EYSENCK

When you purchased this book, it was based on the promise that you would learn the secret of cumulative advantage. Your journey took you from the lofty heights of the global publishing marketplace down into the depths of your reader's unconscious, in between the spaces that can only be seen with an electron microscope. It is here where patterns form that drive our behavior and become our reality. As an author, you can influence a reader at this level and create lasting impressions that the reader can interpret as meeting their human needs for connection, intimacy, and meaning.

With this knowledge, we will build our way up. While this isn't a craft book, you will see how you can use your story to establish a connection with the reader and influence behavior. The more you weave these patterns through your story, community, and communications, the stronger the link will be between your reader and your brand. You can influence the lizard brain and use its unconscious power to change behavior.

DOPAMINE = DESIRE

Our brain chemistry is powerful. The neurotransmitter dopamine is a potent influence on our behavior. Wonder why you procrastinate? Because your short-term distractions deliver a dose of dopamine. If you wonder why it is nearly impossible to pull someone away from social media to purchase a book, it's because of dopamine. Social media feeds do an excellent job of inducing a trance and releasing dopamine, just like snacking, so we fall into this behavior because it is a reliable trigger.

In an experiment, scientists allowed the rat to trigger a dopamine release by hitting a lever. The rat would continue to do this, even forsaking food and water. They also subjected a group of rats to an inverse test where dopamine was inhibited, and the animals weren't even motivated to drink water or eat.[1]

Triggering a neurochemical release needs to be attached to the act of reading your book. This isn't as hard as it may sound if you embed your story with certain activating patterns. Pleasure or satisfaction neurotransmitters drive habit, and by establishing patterns, we can get brain chemistry on your side. You can build a reliable dopamine trigger through pattern matching.

PATTERN MATCHING

While the reader is in a trance state of reading, they open access to the primal association areas of the brain. For a story to work, a reader must engage imagination, memory, and linguistic associations. To do this, we can use to a neurological process that has served our species for millennia – pattern matching.

Our lizard brain looks for patterns. A rustling bush could be a precursor to a lion jumping out of the forest. We seek the cause of an effect. Is the movement from a stalking lion or the wind? We are so desperate to identify cause and effect that we will jump to conclusions with no evidence.

An activator triggers an emotional response that happens at the unconscious level and drives a physical reaction. If a bug flies toward your eye, your eye will shut to protect your vision milliseconds before you consciously process what happened. Before your higher brain functions can draw conclusions and apply meaning, the situation has been influenced by prior learning and emotional associations. These patterns are neural pathways etched into our brains.

In the same vein, we can introduce patterns and link an activator through learning and emotion. In our case, we look to link your characters, themes, sacred words, story, and brand with meeting the character's or the reader's unmet desires (the human givens). Why does a happily married woman read a romance book a day? Is it just for entertainment, or is there a need for intimacy being fulfilled by the pattern of reading romance?

Your words trigger associations, impart experience, feelings, and fulfill needs. The need falls on a spectrum of pure entertainment at one end to meeting an unmet human need at the other end. By focusing on the human givens, your book has a higher probability of triggering an emotional experience. The ultimate step is guiding the reader's thinking about what meaning to apply to this pattern.

There is an expectation for meaning. We humans seek it, and if we can't decipher it, we will make it up. I would argue that William Shakespeare was the Quentin Tarantino of his time: a talented playwright who knew what would draw his contemporaries into the theater. He wrote plays he would want to watch. Did he go to great lengths to imbue all types of hidden meaning and symbolism, or are those interpretations the invention of English professors who are scrutinizing the work? It may be a little of both. The point is that meaning will be applied, either by the playwright or the professor.

Why not use this need for meaning and emotional experience to build a connection? If you're a fan of *Star Wars*, Marvel, *Lord of the Rings* or *Game of Thrones* to the point you think about the characters as role models, or have some personal, internal connection, or hold to a value system you have derived from the story world, then you've created all that meaning and connection in your head. Either on purpose or by accident, *you* created those patterns. *You* recognized this satisfaction (or joy) and applied the meaning.

What I am saying is that as a creator, you should be purposeful in establishing this emotional connection.

HOW DO YOU USE PATTERN MATCHING?

There are ways to implement pattern matching. The first is repeating a known association. If you have already established a pattern or you wish to use one you know is set, then it is a matter of using an activator to trigger that pattern. The real power of the knowledge you have now is to establish new habits related to your story world that will have meaning for your readers.

Let's go through the basics of establishing a pattern. The process will require the following:

> **A trigger:** This can be a sacred word or an action taken by a character; whatever the trigger, look to use it as an activator for a set of associations.
>
> **Learning:** This is the experience. For you, as an author, you need to think of this on multiple levels. At one level are the character's experiences that the reader is living vicariously. This is a powerful teaching method and pattern creation tool you have at your disposal. Then there are the experiences of reading your books, newsletters, and interacting with your community, which can replicate and reinforce the experience of reading.
>
> **Emotional reaction (fulfillment of a human given):** The reader will react and create emotional associations. If they fail to do this, the association they make will be that your books don't work, or *'I don't connect with the characters.'* To make sure you have a high probability of evoking a meaningful emotion, embed your story world, characters, and community with experiences and learning of:

- Security and safety
- Belonging, connection with a broader community
- Status, esteem
- Intimacy
- Attention
- Autonomy and control
- Purpose, Self-actualization

The emotional reaction cements this pattern in the unconscious mind. Your pattern will either mirror an existing pattern in your reader or give them the experience of a new pattern while in a trance state. It is in this trance state that patterns are easier to disrupt and reform. This is the basis of all hypnotic therapy.

Interpretation of meaning: We don't want to leave the meaning of this pattern to chance. You'll help the reader apply the right meaning through your story or metaphor. Show them what the pattern means.

Repetition: Repeating a pattern consistently strengthens the bond between the trigger and the response. We will revisit this pattern matching again when we get to building your community, because there are ways to do this at the community level.

Is there a particular saying (sacred word) that represents belonging or attention in your story world? You can show an arc of a character achieving a sense of belonging, and attach the sacred word to that scene. Later, when looking to attract readers to join your group, you can allude to the circumstances of that scene and close the loop at the community level with the use of the sacred word to signify the reader's achievement of belonging.

Do you have a particular character that exemplifies security, autonomy, or self-actualization? Use your story world, characters, and scenes to establish a pattern of action that results in the feeling and achievement of the primal human needs. Your characters achieving human needs will prime your reader with the imagined experience.

PRIMING AND FLUENCY

It's not just the words you select as a trigger, but words that you associate with trigger words. Your use of language can prepare the readers mind for suggestions. This brings us to the concept of priming. Studies have shown the power of priming[2], and we have already discussed how our brains are associative and designed for pattern matching. By triggering specific associations, you can influence recall and decision-making. We can see this in using word association.

Read the following two-word pairs, and add what word comes to mind.

1. fruit, yellow, _____
2. fruit, red, _____
3. vegetable, red, _____

The most common answers will be banana, apple, tomato. Even though the tomato is actually a fruit, and you may also know this logically, you still might associate "vegetable" with tomato. The point is, we are pre-wired based on our associations to fill in the blank with these items. You have an urgency to complete the task mentally.

If you go back to "Is there a Formula for Recognition and Popularity", you'll see that the quote was by Albert Einstein. I chose that quote to prime you to recognize him in the picture. You can use priming and association in two ways. You can create your priming (sacred words) that align with human givens being fulfilled, or use common priming words that build associations around your brand and story world.

Belonging and connection conjure words that are associated with the feeling of being part of something. Words like *ally, assembly, meeting, couple, congregate, marry,* and *join*. These words have connotations that can help you prime your reader to make the associations you want them to form. When this language is used at the community level or in marketing communications, it will trigger that pattern and recall the desired associations.

Another essential concept is fluency. Fluency is the ease of cognitive processing. The simpler it is for you to retrieve or comprehend an idea, the more positive you will feel about the concept or subject.

Read the two statements below.

"What alcohol conceals, sobriety unmasks."
"What alcohol conceals, sobriety reveals."

These statements convey the same message, but by changing one word and making it rhyme, I have made cognitive processing is easier.

You feel a flow mentally and grasp the idea. The rhyme will also make it simpler to remember.

Fluency for an author starts at the book cover and never stops. The easier you can make it for your reader to comprehend that your book and brand deliver the desired experience, the more positive they will feel about them. Many studies have shown that the more familiar we are with something, the more positive feelings we have of that idea or object. When creating your sacred words, think about how to make these concepts cognitively smooth.

Availability goes hand in hand with fluency. While fluency is about the ease of processing, availability is about the ability to access. Think of it as mental muscle memory – how quickly do we bring something to mind?

Using fluency and availability to improve product sales has been in play for decades. Advertisers have used jingles and slogans to prime us for purchasing. Much of brand advertising isn't a call to action; instead, its purpose is to establish fluency and availability for when the buying occasion arises. They influence you to purchase the product because you are familiar with it.

When it came time for my son to use deodorant, it wasn't because he thought he needed it, but because my wife and I demanded he start using it. The brand he chose was Old Spice. Why? Because he had seen a bunch of YouTube commercials in which the characters just yelled, "Old Spice!" When it came time for him to choose a product, the ads paid off. Priming, fluency, and availability strategies will establish patterns that will become behaviors.

Now, this may sound like PSYOPS and taking advantage of the access you've been given to a reader's unconscious, but the reader will only accept these patterns if there is an unmet need. You have the key, but there has to be the matching lock. Those readers who have unmet needs will get hooked by these patterns that lead to their desires being met. In doing so, you've delivered what your customer wants. How is that a bad thing?

You can also see how the appreciation of your work has less to do with a logical proposition to a potential reader and more to do with connections deep within your reader's unconscious. I call this the emotional payoff. If you can deliver the emotional payoff, then the reader will remember your story favorably and rationalize/remember it in its best light.

The aim is to create associations that are fluent, available, and connected to your brand through icons and sacred words. In your story world, you set the conditioning, and when done right, the reader will be satisfied with the act of reading your book. This is where you win, one reader at a time.

Your writing must also lay the foundation, through pattern creation and matching, to provide triggers to activate the emotions in your community and marketing communications. We will unlock more opportunities and reinforce positive behaviors and experiences back at the mesoscopic level by matching patterns within the community and in your marketing to ones in your story.

In the introduction, I said that your version of this key differs from others that have sought and discovered this key. While the principles are identical, how you weave them into your books, brand, and community will be unique. When done right, the patterns you establish will be invisible to the reader, but you'll know they work because you'll see it in your reviews and communications from readers describing how they connect with the stories and characters. You'll also see it in how your community gathers and grows, building your cumulative advantage.

The reason cumulative advantage eludes most authors is they fail to grasp the vital building block of pattern imprinting and matching. It's counterintuitive that such a minor force as the satisfaction of individual readers should drive a massive force like cumulative advantage. It's easier to think it's all about advertising and search engine recommendations. But just like a landslide is caused by the actions of billions of individual particles of dirt, so to is cumulative advantage an agglomeration of individuals. It is through your story's delivery of satisfaction at the unconscious level that you trigger your avalanche of cumulative advantage.

With what you know now, you can build from the content of your books and individual connection to your work to deliver cumulative advantage. Layer by layer, you can create a positive feedback loop using:

Content: Pattern imprinting and pattern matching within your content.

Brand: Continuity of pattern matching and reinforcement to provide a unified and unique experience.

Community: Content and social reinforcement of patterns, parasocial, and social belonging, recognition.

Virtuous Marketing Cycle: a system to perpetuate the process and accumulate advantage.

UNLOCKING CUMULATIVE ADVANTAGE

11
ZIG WHEN OTHERS ZAG?

> "You want to stand out and be unique and do something different. I always try to zig when they zag - I guess it's a football term, but it applies to a lot of different areas of life."
>
> — SAM HUNT

Together we have looked at research that challenges many of the conventions accepted in publishing. I've also introduced you to novel concepts that can get you to connect with your readers in a profound and meaningful way.

You may have picked up this book because you had already seen for yourself that what used to work for you was no longer delivering results. Maybe you picked up this book earlier in your career to learn from others' mistakes and reduce your pain and suffering. In either case, there is a decision to be made. Do you take this less-traveled path of building a community around your brand? This path requires patience and work. Nothing I'll share from here is a shortcut or hack. No gimmicks or gambits to boost your rank are to be revealed.

I mentioned earlier that a transactional focus results in what I call the vicious marketing cycle. I'll go into depth as to what makes both a vicious marketing cycle, and its antithesis, the virtuous marketing cycle. Before I do that, it's worthwhile to challenge some myths and misconceptions about the market. What can confound you is hearing that these methods are working for others. Most times, they are, and they may give you results faster because they are driven by that vicious marketing cycle. The problem is that over time, you'll exhaust your audience, or you'll become exhausted from learning new tricks, or your business becomes unprofitable as costs rise.

IT'S PAY TO PLAY

If you believe that the publishing market has become pay to play, that's not the worst news. What makes this idea dismal is what it will cost you to play.

In 2019, I spoke at NINC and presented how we are in the early innings of digital advertising's transformation. While Facebook and Google are printing significant profit numbers from advertising, Amazon isn't in their league, but they have no intention of being left out.

An aggressive ad strategy by Amazon wasn't news in 2019. I first began sharing in my newsletter about the changes Amazon implemented back in 2017. While the stock was hitting record highs, it wasn't because they were the world's largest online retailer; they derived eighty percent of profits from the cloud computing division and advertising. When I dug into the retail sales business, they generated more profit from fulfillment for third party retailers than from what Amazon sold. Amazon's strategy to dominate market share had driven most of the profit out of products, and what profit they made, they reinvested in capturing overseas markets. The result: Amazon has never profited from selling products.

In 2017, ads revenue was, by my best estimate, between two and five billion dollars for Amazon. A paltry sum compared to Google and Facebook's ad revenue. How could a company that owns the bottom of the digital sales funnel not make more on ads? Amazon is the number one place for search when someone has the intent to buy a product. Why were they doing so poorly?

Focus.

They weren't focused on advertising. The company didn't even break out advertising as a separate line item of income in the financial statements. That five billion dollars was just shoved in with other miscellaneous income.

That's all changed.

Amazon has focused on advertising. Management has publicly announced their goal to increase ad revenue by five times, and they are on target to achieve that goal. If you've been publishing for the last few years and advertising on Amazon, you've seen the results.

While they have improved tools, they have also increased the space on your sales page to advertise competitive products. While you fight to fix the leaks in your sales funnel with a better cover and tighter sales copy, Amazon punches holes at the very bottom by taking forty percent of your sales page to advertise others' products.

Amazon has also started an advertising division focused on large agencies and direct clients like Proctor and Gamble, Ford, and Nike. While you may struggle with how you can afford to compete with top authors able to spend tens of thousands a month, they are sand fleas of spending when compared to the budget of a multinational consumer goods conglomerate. As these big companies learn the power of advertising on Amazon and other online platforms, more and more of their billion-dollar ad budget will go into digital ads.

I don't believe it is a pay to play market. I'll show you later in this section examples of authors who are doing well with no advertising.

Now, you might argue, *"If they did advertise, they could make even more money."* To some extent, that is true. However, that's not the business they look to run, and they demonstrate that with nearly no ad budget, so they can deliver substantial organic growth.

THE BATTLE BETWEEN APPLE, GOOGLE, AND FACEBOOK

At the time of this writing, Facebook is one IOS update away from their pixel not working on iPhones. Google has already implemented features in Chrome to thwart Facebook. This is all being done under the guise of protecting your privacy, but it is corporate competition in the raw.

Between Apple and Google, they own the operating systems on 95% of mobile devices. Facebook is moving to keep you inside their ecosystem and create an opportunity to sell your wares without leaving Facebook.

Who will shake out on top of this competition for your ad dollars is yet to be seen, but the result will be massive changes to advertising platforms and an increase in the time necessary to learn how these platforms work. To keep up with these changes, you will be in a constant and steep learning curve to make your marketing work. Again, this can be distressing if you're wrapped around the axle of the vicious marketing cycle. Those authors that instead focus on getting closer to their customers will be able to easily transition from where they are today to whatever the future has in store for us.

A RISING TIDE AKA REGRESSING TO THE MEAN

When I first started interacting with the indie author community, it impressed me to see the level of support and sharing within the community. Not that I think it should be competitive, but most industries don't have this level of openness and collaboration. I wholeheartedly support this idea of sharing; however, it comes with some significant drawbacks.

What works today, once shared, loses its efficacy. Early adopters see results, but as more and more apply the hack, its effects fade. Your audience builds an immunity or becomes desensitized to the tactic. When thousands do the same, it dilutes the results for all and regresses to mediocrity.

With advertising, a lot of small, ineffective ads drive up the costs for all. While the obvious result will be low profit, and unprofitable authors will stop running ads, this won't result in flushing out the market. Instead, a constant flow of new, aspiring authors will try to buy into the market and waste precious capital on ads rather than using that money to produce more books.

Is it possible to buy your way to the top of the market? Is cumulative advantage just so simple that those authors who got started earlier and have more money can just spend more?

If you're an author on a limited budget, forget about advertising being your panacea. You, along with every other small author, are bidding on the same keywords and comparable authors. At the same time, there are other top-ranking authors with budgets much higher also bidding on those same keywords. Finally, books don't have big margins so there isn't much extra margin for advertising.

You know from what I've shared in earlier chapters that, more often than not, ads don't scale. Part of the issue is that at the loftiest ranks, the number of sales needed to move from one position to the next are exponential. Moving from a rank of seven to six requires an increase of at least one hundred books a day (depending on the launch season and competition). It was in trying to optimize higher rank summits that I first observed how the consumption of an existing audience drives the rank off of a plateau far more than advertising.

BOY, ARE YOU STACKED

Why are we so quick to assume that some magic promotion combo will lift us up to the top 100? Because in the past, that tactic has worked.

This is another commonly held belief: that a perfect mix of promos, ads, and discounts all stacked together in a small window will whisper sweet nothings to the A9 algorithm and rocket your book up the charts. While stacking promotions can boost rank, it could be at the cost of getting the wrong readers. More likely than not, the result will be a slight rank boost followed by the inevitable pull of rank gravity. As noted above, as more authors come into the market and apply these tactics, the less effective they become.

More concerning to me is the type of business you are building. If the entire sales strategy is built around discount buyers, it will be far harder to break even on a launch. The combo punch of higher costs from stacked promos and ads, combined with heavily discounted books, leaves little money for you.

If you do use a stacking strategy to build your audience, look at what it does to your tail, not how high you ascend at the head of your launch. Retaining readers and getting them to become part of your audience is far more important. As I'll explain in the section about retention in the virtuous marketing cycle, you would be better served by first putting time and money into achieving good retention, then seeing how best to find your audience in new ways.

REDUCED GROSS MARGIN AND IMPACT ON CASH FLOW

Independent publishing changed the game for authors. It wasn't just about getting rid of gatekeepers, but changing the economics. Now, an author is required to take on more responsibility and act as the publisher. An author that could never be picked up by a publisher because the market niche was too small now has the ability to publish themselves and make enough to live on. If your book finds an audience, you don't need to sell as many copies to recover your publishing costs and start making a profit.

Advertising cost increases and a spike in competition are impacting the ability for authors to be profitable. Where in the past, an author would see a 66% gross margin, they may find they now are closer to 30% after factoring in advertising. At this level of profitability, the business may no longer generate enough income to support you full-time. To make matters worse, the advertising dollars are due today, but you don't get the resulting cash for another sixty days. This extended cash flow stress can leave you unable to make payments on all your obligations in the short-term – if Amazon has all your cash to pay for ads, you can't pay your other bills.

IS THERE ANY CORRELATION BETWEEN AD SPEND AND SALES?

You might think I have it out for advertising. To some extent, I do, because I see it as a way that companies like Amazon claw back profits from their partner. The more significant issue for me is that it's not a universal solution. Even with top-ranking authors, results vary. More importantly, as I'll show you here, some top-performing authors are spending far less of their profits on advertising than others.

In the table below, you are looking at some averages and results of authors I've worked with. These are royalties collected, so that sales number would be higher, but I work on monthly numbers to filter out the day-to-day noise.

	Avg monthly Ad Spend	Avg monthly Sales	Return on spend	Correlation
Author A	$8,170	$29,304	3.83x	-0.00005
Author B	$27,260	$95,375	4.00x	0.701
Author C	$6,130	$94,414	23.02x	0.198
Author D	$304	$32,072	537.00x	-0.009

Table 3: Ad spends and correlations

For each author, I've provided the average monthly ad spend and average monthly sales. The number of months in the average varies based on how long I worked with the client, but all are at least eighteen months of data. The fourth column shows the return on spend. All have enviable returns (as the numbers are royalties paid, not sales on the platform). Who wouldn't keep investing when you're getting a three-times return on your money?

In the cases of authors A and B, both felt that ads were an essential factor in their success, but then we ran correlations of ad spend to sales. With Author A, the results suggest absolutely no correlation *or* a slightly negative one. Conversely, Author B had a high correlation. Both authors are, by my assessment, very knowledgeable about ads and, as you can see by the monthly sales, are in the top one percent of earnings in the profession.

These authors had books often going into the top 100, and sometimes the top ten of the entire store, so we were evaluating advertising strategies that could scale. As I stated before, once you get to the top ranks of the store, sales numbers between ranks can require hundreds or thousands more books to be sold per day.

With Author B, we began running detailed analysis during launch, and it was then that I first saw what might be happening. Rather than ad spend driving sales, this author moved ad spend in lockstep with sales, establishing the high correlation. Since this revelation, we have reduced ad spend significantly, resulting in higher profits while continuing to grow sales, not through optimized ads, but by moving dollars previously budgeted for ads toward efforts to build brand and community.

This chart also has good news. Looking at the results for Authors C and D, you can see significant monthly sales that, in one case, deliver on average $384,000 in royalties, and the other, $1.1 million with low advertising. This shows me that advertising, while a tool, isn't a *requirement* for massive success. Both of these authors have a focus on brand and community that results in significant organic growth.

In both cases, the obvious question is would they be even more successful with spending more on ads? To some extent, but I would rather see them stick to a customer-focused brand experience than divert attention to ads and the frustration it often brings.

I can imagine you're skeptical. How is what I suggest different from any other marketing process? Why should you adopt what I readily admit will take time and effort to do, when there appears to be so much evidence that digital marketing, funnels, and ads work for other authors?

In the end, it is your choice how you'll go to market. The vicious marketing cycle has delivered results that I can't refute, nor do I care to because I don't have a vested interest in its success or failure.

What I fall back on is the first principles:

- That all the money in this game comes from readers.
- That readers seek to be satisfied through an experience in your story world.
- If they connect to your story, then your brand will become part of their identity.
- Readers that identify with a brand will follow that brand regardless of where it is sold in the future.

Driving an author business with a virtuous marketing cycle is the solution I've found to create cumulative advantage. Maybe it's better for those who choose to adopt the virtuous marketing cycle that others don't. While they zig, we zag.

12
A VICIOUS OR VIRTUOUS MARKETING CYCLE

> *"Be virtuous and you will be vicious."*
>
> — SAMUEL BUTLER

THE VICIOUS MARKETING CYCLE

Most internet marketing and advertising is conversion focused. Yes, you need to be concerned with closing a sale, but when that becomes the sole focus of all calls to action, your marketing joins the noise that annoys.

Digital direct marketing and high-pressure funnels have influenced book marketing. Many of the early indie publishing pioneers had experience with these strategies and could get astonishing results. Others adopted them because they were working for those a few rounds ahead of them. But once these practices become widely known, they lose efficacy.

The vicious marketing cycle relies on tactics focused on short-term sales, rank, and what is best for the sales platform. It is vicious because it is transactional, not value-creating. It is vicious because it puts the author in a perpetual cycle of learning tactics and processes that may work now, but soon won't.

With each cycle, prior tactics lose efficacy, so more and more time is spent either trying to figure out why the tactic is failing or looking for new tactics. Short-term wins against rank gravity evaporate, and you never have processes in place to indoctrinate and keep fans. Vicious marketing cycles are characterized by the majority of the budget being focused on winning new readers, with little or no budget for retaining existing customers.

Another characteristic of the vicious marketing cycle is reader limbo. Do you leave your readers in limbo between launches? If you have no system to engage and entertain your existing audience, what are they to do once they have made it through your backlist? After a new reader joins your community, do you ignore them until it's time to launch another book?

Without good answers to these questions, you have the problem of reader limbo. Left in limbo, your readers will find other books to read, and never deepen their connection to your brand. What is worse is that this also promotes churn.

Churn isn't an author issue; it's a sales issue. All too often, a business' marketing plan has no budget of time or money for retaining the customer you've already closed. Churn is a measurement of customer turnover.

Mobile phone companies constantly fight churning customers leaving for better deals. A customer that sticks around becomes more and more profitable. Don't you find it ironic that your phone company treats potential customers better than they do existing ones? What if they instead cut ad spend and used that money to reduce your phone bill? I know I would stick around if I knew I would get better and better deals the longer I stayed with a company.

You need a system that ensures a reader won remains a reader for life. Whatever your acquisition cost is, your maintenance cost is lower.

Most book ad gurus can only justify the cost of advertising by looking at read-through. Read-through is just an author's version of lifetime value. By shifting focus away from reader acquisition to reader retention and nurturing, you'll keep more fans and need to win fewer new ones because you can earn more per reader. Your marketing will be more cost-effective when you reduce customer loss. Each reader is part of your principal (more on this concept later in this chapter) that needs to be protected. Furthermore, by keeping a reader, you can enrich the experience of your story world and find those who will spread your message.

THE VIRTUOUS MARKETING CYCLE

The focus of the Virtuous Marketing Cycle is the reader, not the author or the sales channel. The reader is the *sole* source of all economic benefits an author can gain. Without giving readers an expected experience within a story, they won't come back. However, if you deliver on your promise, they will become recurring buyers, and if the bond is strong enough with you, your characters, or the story world, they will adopt it as part of their culture or personal identity.

With the reader at the center, each cycle builds upon the next. Yes, you still have the force of rank gravity acting on your book's visibility, but we design the cycle to nurture readers before and after the launch to reduce churn and deliver an experience. The virtuous marketing cycle should be thought of as a cumulative advantage engine, and its function aligns with how cumulative advantage works.

Authors lose sight of their expectations as a reader; what made them fans of a particular author? No one says an author is their favorite based on their marketing acumen; it is the story and the emotional resonance that captured them as a reader.

Building a culture around your work may seem like a colossal task and something you didn't sign up for as an author. I get it; you don't want to do this, but then don't be envious of those that do and create the fame and fortune you secretly desire.

The novelty of this system is that once you put the infrastructure in place, most of the work is what you love to do: writing impressive stories. While all authors can use this system, each will overlay their own brand experience and story world, so your virtuous marketing cycle will be unique to you. Then, once you get the basics of the VMC in place, it will create cumulative advantage faster because of the underlying behavioral psychology you are using and how social behavior is reinforced by the cycle.

One mindset change is that the suggestion algorithms, advertising, and other marketing tools are amplifiers of your virtuous marketing cycle, not the cycle itself. Search algorithms are important, but not a substitute for the VMC. The secret to "teaching" the algorithm is providing it optimal customer data and then letting it do its work.

What we know about cumulative advantage is it builds over time. It has a social function and requires popularity to perpetuate. Like any compounding effect, it has two primary components: the compounding factor (interest) and time.

Imagine we are building a cumulative advantage savings account. To build up your account value of cumulative advantage, we need to get the components in place and working for you:

1. **The Principal:** This is an initial group of readers. In a savings account, there has to be that initial amount that time and interest cause to grow. Every author starts at zero, so we will discuss how to get that initial slug of readers. The "bank" you'll hold this principal in is your community.
2. **Time:** Your writing career develops over time. If you're planning on earning a living as an author, you intend to have a decades-long career with multiple books. This is where you need to practice patience. In the beginning, it may not feel like it, but you're building cumulative advantage.
3. **The number of cycles (periods):** Within a year, you may have multiple cycles. That number is up to you. It is more important that the sequences are correctly designed than the number of cycles. Over time, you can increase the number of cycles as you gain experience and build advantage faster, but without a properly designed cycle, the system won't work.
4. **The marketing system:** The marketing system is your interest rate. A sound marketing system attracts more readers and keeps them between cycles. Don't get hung up on constructing the perfect system; instead, focus on continuous improvement, making it better each cycle.

There is a lot of work in creating a community and brand experience. If you're early in your career, much of this is tied to story and world-building basics that will spill over into your brand experience.

Now it's time to put this system in place. In the following pages, I discuss the importance and purpose of each phase of the cycle.

13
THE PROCESS

> "All truths are easy to understand once they are discovered; the point is to discover them."
>
> — GALILEO GALILEI

You now understand that the secret to building cumulative advantage is making a deep emotional connection with a reader. Rather than leaving you with the vague idea of emotional connection, I shared a specific system based on the human givens: by using pattern creation, matching, and reinforcement, you can provide a reader with an emotional experience of fulfilling these human givens in your books, and as an experience with your brand and community.

You also understand that you're attempting to transmit a complex contagion, not a simple one. Complex contagions require wide bridges of dense connections where peers reinforce the behavior. Not knowing the actual threshold that causes a trigger, we design for as much reinforcement as possible. You can use brand as a method to bring your story and experience into the real world, blurring the lines between narrative and actual experience. If the brand has sacred words and icons to show the story experience, then readers will associate their identity with your brand. Community will be the foundation for this complex-contagion-spreading network. Through your community, you'll be able to pattern-match and reinforce behavior in reality with peers.

You will need a process to drive the accumulation of advantage. I call the process the virtuous marketing cycle, and I will explain the steps after we dive deeper into content, community, and brand. I explained how the vicious marketing cycle used by most wears out your audience and deafens them to your message. After going through the virtuous cycle, you'll see how it guides you through the consecutive rounds of play to accumulate and use the advantage to your benefit.

Let's begin by looking at the foundation of the connection with a reader – your content.

14

EMBEDDING CUMULATIVE ADVANTAGE IN YOUR CONTENT

> *"You can make positive deposits in your own economy every day by reading and listening to powerful, positive, life-changing content and by associating with encouraging and hope-building people."*
>
> — ZIG ZIGLAR

DO YOU SATISFY YOUR READER?

By deliberately creating patterns or triggering established patterns associated with the satisfaction of human givens, your readers will feel satisfaction.

Why not joy, elation, or love?

Your readers may use those words when describing your book, but the target to hit is satisfaction. Very few things *satisfy* our soul. Most people go through life wanting, feeling something is missing. Your delivery of comfort and contentment is powerful.

Humans spend billions of dollars and hours triggering dopamine releases in meaningless ways. You now have the concepts on why a neurotransmitter trigger aligned with your brand promise can deliver a profound feeling of satisfaction. You should strive to attain this in every book. You must establish a reliable pattern of writing your book (activator), delivering a feeling of satisfaction by giving the reader an experience of meeting a human given, then guiding the reader in how to interpret the meaning of the experience.

Some authors are naturals at establishing an emotional connection with their reader. Pattern matching may shed light on what you have already been doing in your writing. Use pattern imprinting to establish specific emotional connections, and then repeat these patterns in marketing, advertising, and community to trigger those emotions. This may be the part you've been missing.

Pattern matching adds particles of sand to the landslide of cumulative advantage. Each reader you win over increases the magnitude of the landslide and the potential for bigger and bigger avalanches each season. The way this is done is by layering and weaving pattern creation and matching through your books, story world, characters, and community. Therefore, the more you seed your work with patterns that associate words, icons, and characters with the human givens, the more you'll have to hook your audience with.

A word of caution: don't overseed. A shotgun approach to try to be everything to everyone will fail. Start by working with the obvious human givens for your genre.

What follows are some of the most common areas where you can seed, and ways to do it.

STORY ARC, TROPES, AND METONYMS

You build up your patterns from your story. In the state of reading, your reader is in a trance and open to your pattern triggering and imprinting. You are likely doing this already through your story arcs, use of tropes, and metonyms.

> **Story Arc/Pot:** This is the mother of pattern imprinting. Story has always been a method of imparting experience and learning. Frankly, it's the second-best pattern-imprinting process, only following personal experience. A reader observes others (your characters) and learns by their trial and error.

If you dissect your existing stories, do they typically result in your character getting a human given met? You may already practice pattern matching and imprinting. I've found that the authors I work with that are successful either do this unconsciously or deliberately. If you are already doing this, it's just a matter of using what you've already seeded in your community and marketing.

Tropes: Tropes are prepackaged patterns. Through the shared experience of story, we have come to a universal understanding of the meaning of these themes. Using them becomes shorthand to imprint a pattern.

Metonyms: We have a universal understanding of the meaning of specific phrases. "The pen is mightier than the sword" isn't taken literally; it relates to a much higher concept of the power of ideas over violence. Create your own and use these words or phrases in your story and other communications to prime your audience to be emotionally triggered.

Patrick Hanlon explains in *Primalbranding* that groups have a special language that must be learned to belong.[1] If you're a published author, you know terms like KDP and ISBN. Doctors have a language; companies have words that have special meaning. Understanding these words denotes you being part of the tribe, and the use of these sacred words triggers emotion, memory, and associations.

Our cognition is tied to language. We think in word associations. As you read these words, you're drawing on a lifetime of learning and association. Neuro-linguists will argue that your cognitive structure is constructed by the language you learn, and frames your very reality. Creating and using sacred words in your story and community gives you the power to pattern match from your story world into the real one.

The words, "I made him an offer he couldn't refuse," or "Keep your friends close and your enemies closer" are immediately recognizable in pop culture and have sacred meaning to fans of *The Godfather*. When quoted in the real world between two people "in the know," they carry special meaning, bringing the context of the movie's scenes and plot development to an event in the actual world.

Nick Cole and Jason Anspach are the creators of the *Galaxy's Edge* story world. Early in book one, a character mentions the acronym KTF. This acronym acts as an open loop in the story, as you, along with a fresh recruit to the Legion, desire to know its meaning. Not just what the actual letters designate, but the meaning within this band of brothers. The KTF slogan (If you want to know what it means, read or listen to the book) is now on patches and regularly used as a signoff by fans in communications. It has become a sacred word within the community.

You may already have sacred words in your story world. The best are the ones that manifest in the community from user agreement (social convention). But don't wait for this to happen; be intentional and develop sacred words and context.

Your story is the primary place where you can establish sacred words and the related pattern and meaning. Remember, this is where you have an advantage. Your reader's mind is open to establishing new, unique patterns. The more you plan out your pattern matching and imprinting, the more success you'll have when your reader encounters your community or marketing.

CHARACTER ARCHETYPES AND PARA-SOCIAL RELATIONSHIPS

Carl Jung and Joseph Campbell's work shows that archetypes exist across time and cultures.[2] Archetypes, related tropes, and myths relate to how we, as humans, recognize where are human needs, aren't being met, and illuminate a path to rectifying that.

You may already be using story structure like the hero's journey or the virgin's promise to provide structure. These structures resonate because we all are the unlikely hero learning about who we are through the challenges life sends our way. We are all seeking Maslow's hierarchy and the human givens, and without fulfillment of this quest, we don't feel whole.

Your purchase of this book is tied to your quest to achieve something meaningful, becoming the author you know you can be (self-actualization) and having others recognize that talent (status and esteem).

Characters become our role models, acting out their own quests to fulfill a need. If your books are selling, then fulfilling human needs are already part of your writing; now you need to make the connections with your brand and community.

In romance, it's obvious that characters are on a quest for intimacy, but every genre can be laced with pattern fulfillment. The arc of a character fulfilling their quests imprints a pattern in the reader's brain as they imagine the activities.

By setting your characters on quests to attain security and safety, connection to a broader community, status, esteem, intimacy, attention, and control, you'll tap into these patterns that exist within your reader – or, if the reader lacks these, you create these patterns for them. In the process, you create associations through your word choice and how you describe your character's behavior or their interpretation of meaning. Your story allows the reader to complete that quest and establish a pattern of success in the safety of their mind. They associate with the character while seeing your character as a mentor. They get to experience a risky situation without risk.

Through the story experience, the reader creates their own pattern based on co-opting the character's trigger, emotion, and interpretation of meaning. When a character achieves a human given and you write it well, the connection between the reader and the character becomes para-social.

Some of the most vibrant connections a reader can have with your work is a para-social relationship with a character. If you're not familiar with this term, it is a one-way relationship someone has with a celebrity or character. There is extensive research on how friendship and love develop for media figures. This work goes back decades and is foundational to how celebrities can leverage their audiences for fundraising or behavior change through public service announcements.

This connection isn't just limited to actors on the screen; people can develop relationships with fictional characters as well. Researchers have shown there are even cultural differences in para-social relationships with *Harry Potter*. Researchers surveyed readers in individualistic and collectivistic cultures Overall, PSRs and fandom turned out to be quite similar across cultures, with some differences in character perception and relative importance of social attraction. [3]

With the improvements in fMRI, researchers have been exploring how these para-social relationships manifest in the brain[4], observing how sense of self and other referential memory activates in the brain as a person associates with an avatar or character. The study showed a high correlation of activation areas used to store memories of known others. In fMRI tests where subjects were asked to rank personality traits for themselves, close friends, family, and fictional characters where a para-social relationship existed, they measured similar activation for the para-social relationship and known friends.

This was further explored by Ganesh et al (2011), where similar fMRI imaging was used to test comparisons of brain activation and memory recall when thinking of self, others, or the player's avatar. A group of World of Warcraft gamers were given memory tests and asked to rank positive and negative personality traits for themselves and avatars. The recognition memory results showed that the avatar fell between a close other and a distant other.

In survey results and brain activation, a fictional character lives in the same region of the brain as our friends and acquaintances, and we may have a greater emotional attachment to that character than that of a real but socially distant person. As far as a reader's brain is concerned, your characters do not differ from an actual person.[5]

You may be familiar with Meyers Briggs and other personality profiling systems. Some authors use these systems to create character personalities, which determine how they navigate the world. When you combine personality types with a character seeking and fulfilling a human given, you have a complete and complex pattern that readers can connect with. Now a reader can tap into the unfulfilled desire and relate to the character's strategies and reactions on the journey.

A tangent of the personality profile is quizzing your readers to help them identify with your characters. This isn't something new; fan sorting systems have been in marketing for years. Think about the sorting hat in *Harry Potter* and how that plays through to merchandising. What house are you? For a *Harry Potter* fan, this sorting has real meaning.

By the time a reader finishes your book and signs up for your mailing list, they have spent several intimate hours with your character. There is an established relationship to leverage. The more you can blur lines and provide ways for your characters to enter a reader's actual world, the easier it will be for your reader to slip into your community and marketing. Even if you're skeptical about building emotional associations that you can trigger, or you think all a reader wants is entertainment, the fact is, the more your community and marketing look and feels like reading a book, the more comfortable a reader will be joining in and participating.

LORE AND CANON

A rookie mistake for an author is to dump a long backstory or all of your world-building canon into your book to set the stage. If your story world has a rich backstory, and it compels you to share it, then don't overlook how this can be just the content that readers seek. Fans want to know the background and details of your characters and story world. Avid fans will seek this material if they connect with your characters.

By providing this material in original ways, you can keep the reader's interest and identify those readers who are genuinely obsessed with your story world. Lore can be the material that you use in groups and marketing communications.

Lore and backstory are potent tools, and using avenues other than your book is a brilliant way to share this critical information. You can use it as a reward and to signify status and belonging in your community. Bonus chapters, snippets, and other material are great for newsletters, marketing, and rewards for fans.

Keep in mind that what a reader wants most is to read enjoyable stories, so the more your marketing includes added story world content, the easier it will be to get readers to pay attention.

Pattern matching and pattern imprinting are the building blocks of cumulative advantage. It is at the individual level that you connect emotionally with a reader. You can never forget that the reader-writer relationship is where all the value is created. The closer and more durable your connection is to the individuals that make up your community, the more stability you will have in your income.

However, you can't meet all the needs fans will have and keep writing books. You need a more extensive system to nurture the relationship and produce cumulative advantage. This moves us out of the depths of the individual's mind of the microscopic layer, where they consume and absorb content, and up to the mesoscopic realm, where we will design messaging around brand and community to link up to the patterns you create. It is a community where patterns can be reinforced through positive peer pressure to pass on complex contagions.

15

HOW TO CREATE A COMMUNITY THAT BECOMES A FEEDBACK LOOP FOR CUMULATIVE ADVANTAGE

> *"A healthy social life is found only when, in the mirror of each soul, the whole community finds its reflection, and when, in the whole community, the virtue of each one is living."*
>
> — *RUDOLF STEINER*

Once you have hooked a reader with pattern matching, how do you get this individual to create cumulative advantage for your business? We know that cumulative advantage will develop naturally and spontaneously via emergent order. But rather than leaving this to naturally develop, we will guide it.

We have learned that viral marketing is not the right tool. Instead, you need to pass a complex contagion. We need to get a prospective reader to take action and risk to buy and read your book. If this delivers satisfaction, we will require them to do this again and again to become a repeat customer.

Buying books is just the start. Getting readers to passively or actively recruit others is another complex contagion, and the more we do to support and reinforce those behaviors, the better our system will be at cumulative advantage creation.

As I've noted, authors that have been successful at achieving high revenue levels have unconsciously hit upon using community as a cumulative-advantage-building formula. In their case, community developed organically. However, I'm suggesting deliberate organization of a community that creates cumulative advantage. A system that focuses on individual action and acts as a feedback loop to reinforce positive behavior.

You need a system that communicates and reinforces the behaviors you seek. We will build it from two parts: the community, and the virtuous marketing cycle. The community is the human-facing component, and the marketing system drives the process. This means building a community that has strong, extensive ties so that it may pass complex contagions. It will drive sales, but it won't be sales-driven. Instead, it will be purpose-driven, and an experience-focused community.

While your business must sell products to earn a profit, if everything is about selling products, that message gets old fast. If I have bought your latest book and read your backlist, is there a reason for me to stick around? The community must serve all its members where they are at. The community works best when it becomes a living organism.

So how do we do that?

WHAT SHOULD MY COMMUNITY LOOK LIKE?

As you work through this chapter, you may wonder about what this will all look like. Is there an example of a community that you could copy? This is antithetical to the whole idea of building a community. You and your fans need to take ownership, and it needs to be built around your story experience, and what fans want.

If it troubles you that you don't have a logical idea of how your community should be set up, then let it happen organically and listen to what your audience wants. Over time, as you implement the virtuous marketing cycle and grow the community, you'll see that the system will organize naturally. Getting the right people in the community is far more important than getting it systematized and organized. Trust the process.

You have now seen the research showing how our identities are tied to the groups we associate with. We also covered how we build more durable and faster relationships with those who share common interests.

Common interests are one of the leveraging factors to create cumulative advantage, as – Adler and others have proposed – a community need is part of cumulative advantage. We want to share our enjoyment of an artist and converse with those who are "in the know," so we associate with other fans.

Here again, we can leverage the para-social phenomena, this time not just one-to-one, but one-to-many. Para-social connections to a TV series can provide a proxy for social inclusion. We are social animals, and rejection and exclusion trigger emotions that go back to when banishment from a group meant death.

In the modern world, fictional characters and groups can replace real social inclusion and act as a surrogate.[1] If people are so desperate for community that they can create a para-social relationship with a TV series, then you can meet that social need for your readers who have a need to belong.

USING A COMMON PARA-SOCIAL CONNECTION AS THE NETWORK BROKER FOR YOUR COMMUNITY.

Your fans have a universal connector that is intimate with their inner thoughts: your characters. We saw in Milgram's small-world study that specific individuals were vital connectors. One was a Boston tailor that became a focal point for letters to pass through to Milgram's target stockbroker. In the small world you're building, all of your readers have a connection with your characters. Why not use this bond to get them into your group and then help them connect with fellow community members?

FULFILLING A SOCIAL NEED

The community, just like your stories, will be different things to different people. It will need to fulfill the needs of belonging, status, and esteem to deliver lasting value to its members. These are real social needs that, if not met, the reader will look for elsewhere. But if you meet these needs, you'll hook members in a primordial way.

Twenty-first-century society is devoid of community in the way we need it. Social media is a placebo. In a recent IDC survey, 62% of people reach for their smartphone immediately upon waking.[2] We do this as a proxy for connection to the community; we are seeking to belong. Giving your readers a genuine sense of belonging and a way to be part of a group of like-minded people fulfills a human necessity.

BUILDING THE COMMUNITY

You may wonder how much work this will be. If you've been part of a community that works, you didn't see or think about the underlying network structure that compelled your participation. You were drawn to it because of what it did for you, and you wanted to be a member.

Communities that work have typically found success purely out of luck, not deliberate planning. Furthermore, little is done with group structure to promote beneficial behavior. This is where you can be different and design a community with the proper network structure, so it builds on itself, facilitating cumulative advantage.

It is your audience that will be the primary recruiter for future members, not you or your advertising.

This may happen directly through a fan advocating your work, the holy grail of promotion, or through the indirect audience-building that is experienced as cumulative advantage brings notoriety and visibility. A broad audience purchasing the product in a particular cycle increases visibility in two ways: reminding less connected fans of the recent product release, and exposing prospective fans to the product, brand, and community enthusiasm.

Another critical role for your community is reinforcing behavior. This isn't about Draconian rule; preferably, it is using strong social forces to get readers to break through the inertia of not acting. Positive peer pressure and group enthusiasm are powerful behavior modifiers. Look at what people have been willing to do for groups (good and bad).

This challenges the idea of a traditional reader's group. Rather than the group's purpose just being about the lowest common denominator of selling a book, the group allows members to self-select across a spectrum that includes just buying your books, all the way through having a parasocial relationship with characters and socialization with other fans.

To help you understand the best way to design your community, let's talk about bugs.

Examples of perfect behavior-influencing communities surround us. I'm not talking about churches or government. I mean the ant colony. The organization of the harvester ant colony will be our metaphor for the community you'll build.

Harvester ants are a sisterhood. The only time males exist in the society is for the nuptial flight where virgin queens and males are produced and sent out from the colony. This happens the same day every year by all colonies of a certain age. The males don't even have mandibles to eat because they die after insemination.

The virgin queens are produced in the same brood as males and never have prior experience of colony life. They mature and take wing. After the nuptial flight, a fertilized queen will begin her colony. With no help, she burrows down to create a nest and sets out to produce eggs for ten to fifteen years. In the beginning, this queen nurtures the first brood, living only on her fat, then the first brood takes over and organizes into tasks to build and support the colony.

A colony will exist as long as the queen lives, but the queen serves only to produce eggs. The entire colony is her offspring, and they organize into roles spontaneously. It's not like the stories we write where the queen is the royal director of behavior. The queen has never had experience doing the work that her brood will do, and no ant other than the queen lives longer than five years or in another colony. There isn't some Yoda ant that teaches all the other ants how to do things. Instead, the ants self-organize and react to the environment, adjusting roles.

This behavior has gone on for millions of years, the methods and practices encoded at a genetic level. Chemicals and smell are how ants communicate. They leave chemical trails that influence others' behavior. For harvester ants, when the sun rises, scouts begin to patrol. After the patrols are completed, other ants go out to collect seeds while others carry empty husks and dead ants out to the refuse pile.

Experiments where scout ants were blocked from returning to the nest, the foraging ants were delayed. Conversely, when pellets with the scout pheromone were dropped down the entry to nest at a specific rate, the foragers began their activity.

Gordon writes in her book *Ant Encounters: Interaction Networks and Colony Behavior* that studying any single ant doesn't give you much insight, as the behavior seems random. However, studying the colony as an organism, you see the organization and interaction and resilience. [3]

Gordon has spent twenty years studying harvester ants out in the New Mexico desert and has seen how the **colony is an organism** that passes traits onto the next. Gordon observed how, over time, colonies that learned not to forage on the hottest days grew larger and produced more daughter colonies. These daughter colonies exhibited the same behavior.

Somehow this learning is being passed on at the genetic level through a single queen who never took these actions or observed them.

Getting back to building our human colony, the focus tends to be on getting members to join a community rather than designing the system to organize the behavior of the community.

What behavior do you want a new member to demonstrate? If you're an author, it's your community buying more books. However, if all your communications fixate on driving transactions, the group has a weak unifying purpose. Instead, we make the community about serving all the community needs, and in the process of fans getting their needs satisfied, they will be more than happy to bring food to the queen. Not because they feel obligated, but because they see it as a vital role they can perform to keep your colony healthy.

In the ant colony, the largest living mass is the workers. This group spends most of its time foraging and cleaning, while a small portion of the effort is spent on the nursery and the queen. The activities are in service of the community not the queen.

Your first inclination may be to think of sales as foraging, but this couldn't be further from the truth. While sales do nurture you, it doesn't assure the survival of your colony. Your readers are your worker ants, and they need something more than the occasional story to sustain them. They need to have human givens met on a regular basis to continue to do the work you require. The more your community exhibits behaviors focused on mutual need fulfillment, the stronger it will be.

THE HUMAN GIVENS WITHIN THE COMMUNITY

Many of the human givens essential to our well-being are derived from our interactions with others. Here is the list I believe manifest best in the community:

> **Belonging:** There is a human need to be part of something. Our species has survived through social cooperation, and our anxiety and concern for safety are triggered when we don't have a connection with others. Your community can fulfill this need by providing members with a link to people like themselves.
> **Status:** Within a community, we seek status. While we may say we want there to be equality, our lizard brain demands to know where we fall in the distribution of status. We have an innate need to know the pecking order, and we want recognition for our contribution to the well-being of the group.
> **Esteem:** We want the respect and admiration of our cohort. Where status is about how we rank and get rewarded for contributions, we tie esteem to how others value and recognize us.
> Status and esteem can be a powerful motivator in your group. You'll see that the creation of roles and responsibilities will be necessary for your group to become self-sustaining. It is likely that someone in your group is far better at organizing than you; giving them that responsibility within the group, that status, grants them recognition and reward, the ensuing esteem. Incentives such as free books, swag, and good old cash for services rendered are all worthwhile if it gets your community organized.
> **Attention:** We seek attention. When the group gives its attention, members are validated. We also seek the attention of those we

respect. This can be members of higher status within your group, or…you.

Autonomy and Control: While people seek to be in a group, they don't want to be ruled. Groups thrive when there is a sense of autonomy for their members, and they feel they are in control. The more you can create a "choose your own adventure" feel for your fans, the more they will self-select into roles they are comfortable filling. The more they feel they are organizing and managing the group, the further they will commit to doing the work for the group to thrive.

How much autonomy will you allow? There are risks with how much you provide, but also significant rewards. The Grateful Dead allowed fans to record live shows then trade and profit from those recordings. While frowned on by the majority of musicians, this resulted in The Grateful Dead being one of the most profitable bands, and with a die-hard following.

Purpose/ Self Actualization: One of your secret weapons is to provide ways for members to fulfill social and personal psychological needs through interacting with your community and brand. Helping them to understand their worth and achieve their goals will show the value of your brand, community, and content. Here you can tie the reader's identity to your brand identity through helping them fulfill a purpose within the group.

BECOME A SOCIAL NETWORK DESIGNER

Those who learn how social networks are structured can build networks that deliver results. In my research, I've been looking for the solution to building cumulative advantage – the "how-to" of cumulative advantage hasn't existed until this book. Creating a network that increases the probability of building cumulative advantage is the end goal.

Remember the thought experiment of a forest and lightning? The analogy is fans are trees and a launch or media post is the lightening to trigger the fire (contagion) to be spread. In it, we looked to improve our likelihood of our tree being hit from one to two percent. While small, that is a one hundred percent increase of each tree being struck.

The chances further compound when you look over a series of seasons. Over ten seasons, there is now a twenty-percent chance of that strike, and because our network (forest) has propagated further, that fire will spread faster. The small probabilities compound over rounds to create higher probabilities of success. The way to create this probability is with your network design.

Community and brand are a means to make participation fun and user-friendly. You will be running a social experiment, so you'll need to learn from what the experiment shows you, and make improvements along the way. But don't leave it to spontaneous organization for your community to form. Take inspiration from the harvester ant colony and design roles, activities, and signals that trigger behaviors of the community, then reward members with recognition, status, purpose, and items of value.

To create this environment for your readers, it may help to get some network basics under your belt. This isn't meant to be an education on the dry and sometimes confusing topic of network design. The purpose is to give you insight into the essential attributes of a social network structure, and make sure yours has the necessary qualities.

Let's begin with connections. Each person in a network is called a node or vertex. I'll be using the term 'node'. The connection between two nodes is an 'edge'. Edges can be directed or undirected, meaning there could be directed communication from node A to B, designated by an arrow to B, or back-and-forth connections with no arrow identifying direction.

You can see in the graphic that there are three nodes – A, B, and C – and there are edges between A and B and B and C.

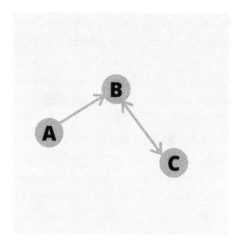

Figure 21: Sample Network Diagram

Nodes and edges are the building blocks of a network diagram. As we learned earlier, edges can be weak or strong ties, designating the type of relationship. Is this person just a fan that lurks in a Facebook group, are they someone you regularly connect with via email or Messenger, or are they a friend who is also a fan?

Defining weak and strong ties in your network is qualitative. The point is, you need to know what strong and weak ties look like, and not only between you and network members. What constitutes a strong tie within your network?

As I said earlier, this is part social experiment, and as the researcher, you must observe what makes up a strong tie, and the characteristics you can attribute to the node or edge. Are there roles, activities, or attributes you can Identify?

Now, you may say, *"I don't have time to do this; I didn't sign on for this as an author."*

I understand this position, but if you leave that behind and open yourself to doing this work, you'll see it isn't as hard as you think. What I'm suggesting isn't a clinical experiment; instead, while building a fun community, you'll observe the characteristics of what works and what doesn't. Once you see these patterns, you can scale the system to replicate and reward those who show those behaviors.

This may be the only way you'll ever be able to scale your business. If that's true, then your choice to *not* do this work is to choose failure.

Your network is your business in many respects. You'll have a peer network that can help you with marketing and professional support. You have a reader network that is best exemplified by the community you build. As your network builds, clusters will develop. What makes a cluster? Natural grouping around common traits. There will be clusters within your network, and your network itself is a cluster or subset of larger networks, such as users of Facebook, Goodreads, or SciFi-convention-goers.

A cluster can be measured by density, which is the number of edges within the cluster. High density means the members have more interconnected relationships. This is an important quality we will look to foster. The density of strong ties creates the wide bridges you need to get the complex behavior of a sale and future participation to happen from a new member.

Clusters and networks will organically grow; this can hurt us or help us. It all boils down to how your network evolves. Is it random, or guided by your intentional design?

HOMOPHILY AND HETEROGENEITY

I'm a proponent of understanding your customer segments. You can customize what you offer to their tastes and extract more value out of those who are prepared to pay more for added value.

Beware, there is a pitfall. In looking for the differences, you can lose sight of the commonality. Conversely, make sure you understand these differences to understand how groups may need to be treated differently.

Let me give you an example.

A client of mine began selling swag boxes with signed books. Before launch, we surveyed her mailing list and determined that $40 was the threshold for a box price, but with low interest overall. She ended up creating two boxes: one at $40, and another at $100, which was going to be for giveaways to fans during launch. She decided to run a preorder aligned with her latest book launch to see if there was interest in these, but was prepared to give the boxes away as promotions if the preorder didn't go well. The preorder opened with a message to her Facebook group.

She ended up selling most of the $100 boxes in a few hours.

When the boxes were presented to the mailing list, only a few from the $40 category sold. Our survey was correct, but we didn't survey all of her community, specifically the online group who proved to be prepared to buy at a higher price point.

Learn the commonality and differences of your community.

Community-building is the backbone of cumulative advantage. We should first and foremost focus on what all our readers have in common, for this is what we can build the community around so members will see a bit of themselves in others. Help new members see why they belong and how they have found their home.

Craig Martelle is a bestselling, six-figure-earning author. Along with producing fiction for his personal fans, he has built one of the largest communities of authors with Michael Anderle. In speaking with him about how he was able to build the group so fast, he made it very clear that he had a unifying message: the group was for authors looking to make money selling books. He would set a buffet of ideas, concepts and methods to help authors seeking to profit from writing, and it was up to each of them to pick up what works for them.

That unifying message both attracts and deters. The group is not meant to be everything to everyone, but those who join and feel that the group is the right fit immediately recognize the value.

In building your community, you will also need to define who the group is for and understand that it won't serve everyone's needs. You seek both a diverse and similar audience. The ideal mix is a community as diverse as possible, with the commonality (homophily) being your content.

Think about how diverse the fan base is for a sports team. Having community members with diverse backgrounds provides an impetus for organic growth. The more varied the group, the harder it will be to build out dense network bridges, but those bridges have a higher probability of reaching new, untapped markets.

I mentioned earlier an excellent example of the growth that Andrzej Sapkowski's work garnered when the series released on Netflix. Many of the new content consumers would never have known about his content because they wouldn't pick up a book or play a video game. Similarly, authors are tapping into other consumers through audiobooks – consumers that don't read but love to hear stories.

Similarities and differences also require that we talk about the associative and dissociative attributes of a group. Many groups define themselves by what they are and what they are not. This is heavily present where I live, in Chicago. A Cubs fan is not a Sox fan, and vice versa, but they both can be Bears, Bulls, and/or Blackhawks fans. Sometimes the rivalry can be healthy; sometimes, it is divisive.

While I believe that politics and religion are best left out of the conversation, you may not. Making the conscious choice to use a dissociative feature has proven to be effective. Maybe your work is politically charged and appeals to one segment while enraging another. Building your echo chamber may be a good commercial decision. However, understand that in doing so, there will be a portion of the marketplace that will have negative emotions associated with your work.

I've concluded there are three traits to a successful group, and you must have at least one:

Associative: People want to be included with those like themselves. This is a core trait of the community that you build. People will look to associate with your community and like-minded people seeking a social component of your brand. You can use your creed, sacred words, and rituals to cement a person to the community, where they'll see traits in themselves in other members. When this is done right, they want to be part of this community because it completes their identity.

Aspirational: Some groups have an aspirational aspect. People join because they seek to be like the others, but don't feel they are worthy. The common aspiration to a goal drives groups focused on transformation.

Many of us read to be inspired. We love to see a character face their flaws to overcome a situation and, in that process, find their strengths. Your characters can be that inspiration and help others get to where they can discover their strengths. Creating an aspirational component to your community is a hard link to purpose and self-actualization.

Dissociative: No one wants to foster divisiveness… or do they? For some, it's not just what you love, but what you hate. Ask a sports fan about a rival team in the league; while no one wants to incite divisiveness, sometimes it can help to focus the group.

With *Harry Potter*, there are various houses. Fans are associative with other fans, yet can have a healthy and fun rivalry with opposing houses.

Some of the most powerful moments in history (for good or bad) have used a dissociative element to create an 'us versus them,' pulling the *us* closer together.

These are all tools to get your fans to connect, collaborated and experience your brand in a fulfilling way. From time to time you'll have products to sell them that they will willingly buy. With the community built your ABC (Always Be Closing) days are over.

UNDERSTANDING NOT APPLYING PRESSURE

Too often, groups pressure rather than persuade. If we understand what others want, then it becomes easier to get what we want, either by finding mutual benefit or by using what the other seeks to persuade them to get what we want.

All of your readers fall on a spectrum of desiring entertainment (mindless or otherwise) to try to fulfill an unmet human need. Give them what they desire as the reward for the activity you want. By using pattern matching, you can attract readers to the behaviors you seek.

For example, if you're seeking candidates for managing your community, create a position of status and make sure you acknowledge the status personally and within the group. Never forget, the more ownership group members have, the easier it will be to get them to manage processes.

SIGNALING AND TRIGGERING BEHAVIOR

Like the ant colony, there needs to be a system of communicating what behavior and roles members can play. In the harvester ant colony, ants fill the roles of scouts, foragers, clean up, tunnel construction, and nursery care. Younger ants begin in roles inside the mound and closest to the queen. They naturally adjust roles based on need.

When looking at the behavior of our ants, there is a threshold trigger. As the scouts return, foragers forage. If foragers return at a higher rate, then cleaner and construction ants will break off and begin foraging. The frequent return of foragers signals to the sisterhood there is a close or abundant food source, so the colony takes advantage of the opportunity to hoard more seed. This isn't coordinated; there is no ant control tower dictating behavior, only the frequency of pheromones entering and exiting, eliciting a reaction in others.

This idea of behavior patterns and triggers to guide and allow members to self-organize is foundational to your community. In designing your community after the harvester ant colony, we're not looking to create a hive mind, rather an embedded system where constituents signal to each other, trigger behavior, and adopt roles that suit them.

Think about when you see a signal from another like-minded fan. If your favorite band is Rush and you see someone wearing a Rush 2112 T-shirt, you think about them differently. You may even talk to them, although they are a stranger to you. *The brand has acted as a social catalyst for you and another to define your interaction.*

You are trying to be this catalyst, creating patterns that trigger behavior between fans at the microscopic layer to trigger and reward behavior within the community.

You'll need to map out some activities and roles for community member participation. This should include how a community member takes on the role. Design roles to be self-selecting and self-starting. The more community members can exert autonomy and self-control, the easier it will be for the right person to receive the signal and pick up the work they are best suited to do.

You'll also look to align signaling with your virtuous marketing cycle.

What behaviors are you looking for members to act out, and when? You want them to help you promote your new book, so providing them a post to share seems like an obvious action. Some will do it. However, helping them celebrate the latest book in a favorite series with other fans is far more fun for them, and if planned right, can lead to far more organic reach from the buzz fans create sharing personal wins and what they are proud of.

WHAT ROLES DOES YOUR GROUP REQUIRE?

Here are some examples of roles you may have in a community and how to support them.

> **Lurkers:** People that join but don't actively take part will be a large part of your community, usually the largest. While implementing community strategies will encourage and reward participation, most members will be quiet. This is a natural part of the process of people warming up to the group, and should be supported and acknowledged. Having the community pay attention to those that are less active builds their comfort and can bring them to be willing to participate.
> **Greeter and onboarding:** Having someone who takes on the responsibility of helping a new member get oriented will go a long way to getting higher participation and retention. This becomes the first step in helping your community identify behavior and signal to each other what is expected. This can include conduct codes, but that shouldn't be the sole content and focus. Instead, this should be about helping recent members get value out of the group through their contribution or by interaction with others. Sometimes using the para-social relationship that your members have with your characters could be the best way to onboard.
> Years ago, I was a member of a martial arts gym. After not attending for a few weeks, I received a call from one of the instructors that knew me. Part of their practice was a weekly staff meeting, where they went through a list of people that

hadn't attended a class for two or more weeks. Instructors would then volunteer to call those on the list just to check in. When I received that call, it made me feel that they cared and I was part of the club. It was a brilliant move for retention to keep my monthly fees coming in the door.

Community manager(s): Some of the most successful groups use a community manager that isn't the author. This keeps the author's personality out of the management process. A community manager that is a fan is also more relatable by the community. Besides keeping you out of community management, this separation of roles makes your engagement in the group more valuable.

This is a crucial role in your community, so finding someone with passion and commitment is imperative. When you get this person, don't skimp on rewarding them. Early in your career, when you don't have as many resources, make sure you recognize and reward this person with exclusive access, insider information, and other compensation tied to esteem, attention, intimacy, and belonging. Later, when money is flowing, don't leave this person out in the cold. Financial compensation for a worthwhile community manger will be a better use of your money than advertising spend or a virtual assistant.

Local leaders: Development of geocentric clusters helps to bring your community further into the actual world. Martha Carr has built a strong following by meeting with readers when she travels. Her process centers on a fan lunch, which she pays for, and she brings swag. Most of the lunch is just hanging out with her readers.

I've observed one of these events and seen the power. People traveled for hours to get together and just socialize. We spent very little time talking about the books; mostly, we were getting to know each other, and strengthening the group's bonds.

This was the building of strong links and dense clusters in action. Even if the group never gets together again, that one event created the connections that facilitate community growth and the reciprocity for those fans to advocate on her behalf.

This is not a comprehensive list, but it gives you some ideas of the roles you can create to make your group autonomous.

BUILDING SUB-NETWORKS

Within your broader community, there will be sub-groups that have special purposes. Use membership to these groups to help your marketing as well as highlight status and belonging.

> **Beta Readers:** If you're not familiar with the term, beta readers are people that get to read your work before its commercial release. They are part of the quality control process and provide feedback and criticism to reduce the potential of a commercial flop. The beta reader group is a cluster within your community that has special responsibilities. Make sure they are acknowledged for their contribution.
> **Street Team:** The street team is a term used by some authors to do launch promotion. This can include social media posts, reviews, and other acts of support and social proof. The more you make launches and promotions celebrations for your community, the better participation you'll get.
> It has been my experience that investing in promotions in your existing community delivers long-term results of advantage-building. Giving your promotion money to your community pays dividends compared to giving that money to an advertising platform. If you celebrate with your fans, you may not need a street team in the traditional sense, because this becomes expected behavior during a launch cycle. Instead, your community becomes a de facto street team during launch. When signaled, all help promote and participate in the celebration. When your favorite band goes on tour to support its new album, you see that as an opportunity to go to an event with fellow fans and have a live music experience. From the band's perspective, they are onstage earning money and promoting album sales. How can your launch events be made into experiences rather than a process to get reviews and rank?

Content Creators: While you love to create content related to your story world, you may bristle at creating content for a community. Permitting, promoting, and rewarding community members for creating content will reduce your workload.

We are all biased to like and take ownership of what we create. It is known as the Ikea effect. Give your community the latitude to create fan fiction, memes, and polls to reduce your need to produce material, and allow them to feel that they have ownership of the community.

The Inner Circle: The fans with direct access to you. Most never use it, but having that status is meaningful. Having smaller groups where they have intimacy with you is an excellent reward for those who have taken on community responsibilities. This inner circle should be made up of a representation of other subgroups and act as your one place to get feedback and direct what you want to have happen in subgroups and the community.

IDENTIFY THE MOVERS AND SHAKERS

Within the community and these sub-networks there will be people like Milgram's Boston Tailor that was a key connector. Folks like this are priceless because they straddle the strong and weak tie. They are what Ron Burt calls brokers, as they have the ability to connect across gaps in others networks.[4]

Some people have all the connections. Centrality is the idea that specific nodes have more connections. You'll notice this in social situation; certain people just seem well connected. Identify those who bridge clusters and like to broker relationships, and engage them to do this for your community. By acknowledging them and rewarding them, you'll get them to be even more active at something they are already good at. My experience has been that these connectors excel in the roles of onboarding and local-cluster-building.

GROUP IDENTITY

An enormous part of belonging is knowing what the group is and what it stands for in the world. This aligns directly with your brand promise, rituals, and associative and dissociative features of the group. Specifically, it provides an identity for the community and the subgroups that associates with your story world. Do your characters hang out at a particular bar? Or do you have functions like mercenary groups or some hierarchy that can give your fans the ability to link their identity with that of your story world?

What behaviors do you want your group to take part in?

SELF-DIRECTED BEHAVIOR

You now understand the value of the human givens. Within a group setting autonomy is an important need. No one likes to be told what to do. Instead, stay focused on the draw of experience, status, and belonging to direct their behavior. Let users self-select and explore what you offer. This gives them a feeling of autonomy and control. Along the way, educate them on how they can gain recognition, status, and a deeper belonging to the group. This should begin when a reader signs up.

BEHAVIORS AND ACTIVITIES

Creating activities and managing behavior isn't just about policies around discussing politics or religion (though of course, you must maintain civility); it is also about establishing the core behaviors and processes that facilitate a robust community. Like the ant colony, there are roles to serve that keep the community as a whole healthy and safe. Within these roles, there are behaviors and signaling, just like with ants, to start others' actions.

Here are some key areas to focus on:

- Indoctrination and Onboarding
- Engagement and Entertainment

- Launch Celebration
- Management

Indoctrination and Onboarding: This is by far the most essential process for your community. When a new member shows up, how are they treated? For most, this is viewed as a necessary evil instead of a vital bonding process that sets the tone for future involvement. Your onboarding can drive your retention by making the process of joining the group fun and engaging.

How easy do you make it for users to become community members, and what incentive have you provided?

Consider this; your reader is coming out of their reading zone, a trance state where they were deep in memory and imagination. If they have connected with your story world, they would like to continue this experience. How can you extend the experience and shift them to take action in the real world?

Use your story world, characters, or author persona to do the work. A reader still in the trance state could be asked by your character to help fulfill a quest with the reward of more story content; that would be one way to bridge from the part of the brain where your characters live to the actual world.

The point to absorb here is to avoid going full salesman, and use experience and mystery to draw your reader into your community.

The common indoctrination practices are a four to six-email sequence that ends in "buy my books," with occasional requests along the way to join a group or follow a page. This can work, but again, your indoctrination will be like many others, and it is transaction-focused. Get into the shoes of your prospective fan and see the process from their perspective.

When a new member comes into the community, they are cautious and excited, looking for validation that the risk they just took will be worth it. For a reader to complete your book then sign up for your newsletter is a big commitment, so if they make an even more significant commitment to join a group, they need to be recognized.

The unknown member is self-conscious and concerned about offending you or the community. Having a host and an onboarding process is critical to get the newbie through this phase and retain them. And having trusted fans do onboarding work is essential for two reasons. First, greeting everyone will become a full-time job. Second, members of the group will be forging strong ties that bind, and we now know these are the connections our fans need to know how to form. Having a process that establishes the pattern of building strong ties will promote the behavior inside and outside of the group. By using a fan to do this you set up the behavior you want right from the start.

For community-building, the indoctrination sequence needs to be about how the new member can get the most out of the community. While orienting them to how they can get value out of their membership, you can help them assimilate and get comfortable taking part in the group. Use examples from your stories and characters to help drive the point home. Create icebreakers and ways to get a reader to speak up about what is attractive to them.

Engagement and Entertainment: By providing engagement and entertainment between your releases, your fans never stray too far from your brand. If they are always engaged at some level, then retention is more natural.

If you're an author putting out a book a month and wondering if you can ever get off that treadmill, this is your saving grace. With planning, you can shift to fewer launches, and use your ability to write fast to keep your fans close with exclusive group content that warms them up for upcoming books. Using your mailing list, you can keep them engaged and reading while you transition to a less grueling schedule.

Never forget your fans are readers; they want to have their nose in a book, so giving them stories is the most valuable gift you can provide. Use serialized content, backstories, and lore to keep readers entertained and feeling part of something special.

Polling: Want to get your fans excited? Ask them what they want to see more of in your story world. Getting feedback can help you get out of your head and hear what your readers desire. It also makes them feel more important, and enables you to deliver what the market wants.

User-Generated Content, and the Ikea Effect: Letting fans provide content in the group triggers the Ikea effect (you value more what you create) by giving them the feeling they have influence and input into the creative process. This also reduces what you personally have to provide to the community for content.

I know for some there can be concern around the ideas of copyright and intellectual property; I lean toward protecting the assets versus letting fans have free rein. However, there are ways to do this with licensing, and giving fans this autonomy goes a long way toward tying their identity to your brand. But you have to be comfortable with the latitude you give fans for creating content in your community. Is it just memes and fan-related commentary, or do they have some authority to create work derived from your intellectual property? If you want to have fans cosplaying your characters or making 3D miniatures, then you need to support and embrace the behavior.

The Four Horsemen Universe is a military science fiction series that is one of the fastest-growing brands in the genre. It does so because of inclusivity. This may have been born from the spirit of the founders, as it has always been about the collaboration between several best-selling sci-fi authors. Each year, they have at least one anthology that features new and veteran authors.

The Four Horsemen Fan Club is autonomous and run by the fans with its own corporate structure. For many, it would be unheard of to allow fans to have such latitude with intellectual property. I have to admit, when Chris Kennedy first shared this with me, it shocked me, but this comes from a perspective of ownership and asset protection rather than allowing the fans the ability to belong and create the value.

Fan fiction, cosplay, and fans creating clubs are behaviors that demonstrate their wanting to belong. They feel they have ownership because your words came to life in their imagination. In some respect, they *do* have ownership, as their head is where the stories play out, with their biases and associations filling in the details.

Another fiction-based fan club is The 501st Legion. Known as Vader's Fist, the 501st is a *Star Wars* fan club where members are part of a stormtrooper legion. Members have numbers, and cosplay and do charity events. This club has been so rabid in its support of fandom that Lucasfilm has included the 501st into the official material and canon.

Another important lesson about belonging and The Four Horsemen example is that Chris Kennedy and the other authors could have put a ton of work into making a fan experience that they thought the fans wanted only to have it fail. However, by giving the fans the freedom to craft the experience, the club delivers what they want.

That may just be what's at issue; authors are focusing on what *they* want rather than what community members desire.

Rituals: What acts do fans take part in, and what do these acts mean to them and the group? Creating routines and activities to celebrate being part of the group can formalize inclusion and belonging. This could be as simple as signing up for your newsletter, or as elaborate as a convention of fans. When certain fans rush to finish a book first and look to discuss the latest events, that is a ritual. Rather than letting this be an ad hoc process, formalize and celebrate it with those fans looking to participate. Have mini celebrations and rituals around completing onboarding and launching books, and reward and acknowledge positive behavior.

Rewards and Recognition: Just like with a child or puppy, you need to reinforce the behavior you desire. My word of caution is not to make this all about reinforcing sales processes. Focus on support behaviors like indoctrination and retention. Getting the community to take care of its own and support the hive garners better results for the queen.

Reward is all about closing the loop on pattern matching behaviors. A few things about rewards: they have to be delivered as close as possible to the requested action, and they need to be of value to the audience you want to attract. The colossal mistake that many make here is they focus on items like gift cards and Kindles, but these types of rewards attract the wrong folks to your community. Die-hard readers want stories and insider information.

Launch Celebration: This work is all about building an audience that will deliver cumulative advantage. You're running a publishing business that needs to sell books – better still, more and more books with each release. Have a philosophical shift, and make launches about anticipation, joy, belonging, and fun.

Enough of the talk about conversion, cold and warm audiences, and advertising optimization. Do you like to be sold that way? I don't, and I cringe when I see it has overtaken an author's marketing. Make each launch a time for those fans who support you to get excited and celebrate. Reward and recognize them when they help.

I've worked with several authors who have built up a significant social presence by running contests with their closest fans. Reward those who help you get the message out, and use reader-generated content whenever possible.

Management: Unlike our ant colony, your fans won't have behaviors wired into their DNA. Instead, you need to use community managers and roles to guide the group to act out the behaviors you seek. Peer pressure is a powerful force (for good or bad); be sure to use it to get the behaviors you want and don't want. You'll be surprised how quickly the groups and subgroups will organize around these behaviors as long as you establish enforcement. The more these can be system-influenced behaviors – essentially social conventions, and not enforced by edict – the faster you'll see their adoption.

All of this is general guidance for building the community that suits your brand. The beauty of this system is, while structurally similar to other authors', your group will have a different look and feel because your brand is built off of your story world.

From here, we will explore how to design your brand around your story and the desires of your readers.

WAYS TO DEFINE YOUR TRIBE

Origin Story: If you're of a certain age, you watched *The Brady Bunch* on television. If you take a moment to think about the opening jingle, *"Here's the story of a lovely lady..."* Does the rest of the song come to you word for word? Do you remember the gist of the jingle? In that quick intro, they gave you the origin story: a woman with three daughters married a man with three sons. Then each episode was a different tale featuring the various cast members, but it was all tied together around this idyllic, blended family.

An origin story can take on mythic proportions and become dogma. The easier you make it for the community to repeat and reinforce it to each other the quicker it will become mythic.

Do you have an origin story? The story can either focus on you as a content creator, or tie in to the story world. But having an origin story that can be communicated almost like an elevator pitch helps the community understand why it exists, and helps members communicate the tribe's defining ideas to others.

The Creed: A creed is a way for your fans to validate what fans believe. This can be the brand promise or some ideals you and your fans share. You want to have a core understanding condensed into words that your fans can repeat to others to share your message or confirm that others are part of the group.

The Icons: What are the symbols of your brand? What do they mean? Rather than leaving this to luck, or letting them be revealed over time or even chosen by fans, you can be deliberate in creating icons and placing them in your story. Just as you use symbols and metaphors in your story, it should ooze into your brand.

16

WHAT IS YOUR BRAND PROMISE, AND DO YOU DELIVER?

> *"When a company owns one precise thought in the consumer's mind, it sets the context for everything and there should be no distinction between brand, product, service and experience."*
>
> — *MAURICE SAATCHI*

If you're one of those authors who is hesitant to build a brand around yourself, then I have some splendid news. Your fans aren't that interested in you as a brand either. Let me clarify; while you can do this, and your author name can become a trigger for your brand promise – meaning seeing your name activates associations that the reader has patterned from reading your books – that brand-building can be limiting. If you follow this path, remember that you are still creating perceptions about what your author name means, and it's not *you*, it is the reader's perception of you, and that brand fantasy needs to be crafted.

I believe the more natural path for authors is to blur the lines between the actual world and your story world. Does a *Star Trek* fan have stronger feelings for Gene Roddenberry or Captain Kirk? For that matter, are those feelings stronger for the character Kirk or the actor (pick yours, Shatner or Pine)? Rather than focus on creating one more character (the author), use the characters you've already invented. You've done the heavy lifting in your book. If you have used characterization and story arcs to have your characters show pattern matching, then para-social relationships are already formed. Use these relationships to your advantage, as your reader has a personal, intimate relationship with the characters you create. If done right, they have been in the character's head, and the character is literally in theirs.

BRAND PROMISE

Take some time to create your brand promise. Think through how it ties to human givens and your story world. Having a written brand promise to reference will act as guidance as you build out your brand and community.

Where the promise has to come to fruition is in your stories. Without deliberate effort to deliver on your brand promise, you'll never get fans to obsess about your work.

You have more control over this than you might think. It's not about look or logos; your brand manifests itself when a reader begins to read your words and imagines the story you are weaving. No other product has the potency to connect faster with a user than a story. The connection a reader has is personal and tied to their own identity when it links up to unmet human givens.

BRAND FANTASY

Along with writing out your brand promise, think through the human givens that are associated with your brand. The emotions you want brand users to come away with, along with the experiences you want readers to enjoy. Delivering that satisfaction is what makes the brand fantasy real for a fan.

Dissect some of your favorite story brands. Think about how they make you feel. Map out what causes you to feel that way. Is it the characters, the story world, the story arc? Look to how the brand triggers your emotional reaction, and why you feel satisfied.

Deconstructing your favorite brand fantasy can help you build your own.

A BRAND BIBLE

Capturing ideas to remind yourself of the meaning of your brand might seem like extra work, but in the process, it will help you get clarity on how your brand fits together. Remember, if you can't articulate the brand fantasy, then how will a fan ever be able to do it? You want your brand and its promise to become dogma amongst your fans.

What pulls all of this together?

If you have a coherent strategy about your brand and building a community, and you tie everything together with patterns that are wired to fulfilling human givens, will cumulative advantage fall from the heavens like mana?

No. There needs to be a system that drives the accumulation.

A big part of cumulative advantage is participating in round after round in this game called publishing. We need a process that makes sure you are optimized for each round by applying the resources you have accumulated in previous rounds. You likely already have a system for marketing. With some adjustments, we can change it from a vicious marketing cycle to a virtuous one.

17

MAKING IT HAPPEN: BUILDING YOUR CUMULATIVE ADVANTAGE ENGINE

> *"There is no scarcity of opportunity to make a living at what you love; there's only scarcity of resolve to make it happen."*
>
> — WAYNE DYER

In this section of the book, you will see suggestions for each step for creating your virtuous marketing cycle (cumulative advantage engine).

The macroscopic level, where cumulative advantage manifests and feeds back to influence a wider group of individuals, is driven by our work at the mesoscopic and microscopic levels. The following framework can help you build your system.

General Concepts:

1. The publishing market is heavily influenced by cumulative advantage.
2. Your advantage accumulates over time.
3. This is a game of multiple sequential rounds or seasons.
4. In each round, we look to accumulate more advantage and consolidate the base.

5. A system that *conserves* and accumulates will compound advantage faster.

THE VIRTUOUS MARKETING CYCLE

Start: This is an initial priming step. A one-time phase where you establish your foundation and create principal for compounding. If you already have an audience (any size), consider this done. You just need to craft your virtuous marketing cycle to compound. If you're just getting started, there is an initial period that you need to go through to get your starter audience.

Launch: Every cycle will have a launch associated with it. While this part may feel a lot like the vicious cycle launch, you'll see differences in what happens in the sales channels, the language you use in advertisements, and other promotions you trigger.

The first twenty-one days of the launch set the momentum, then rank gravity takes hold as your existing and new audience works through the book. You will attract new readers during the launch, but while you've sold them a book, you now need to keep them.

Accumulate: Each round – or launch – you accumulate new readers. Using behavioral psychology principles, we seek to get them connected with your brand experience and community.

After launch, you need a system that builds your community and promotes readthrough, giving those who enjoy your creations a way to connect and continue the experience of your story world and brand experience.

This phase is a fundamental difference. No longer are you just pushing updates, but creating a social network that is reader-centric and structured to deliver the benefits of a community. In the book *People Powered*, Jono Bacon's research shows how a customer community can become a value creation system.[1]

. . .

Indoctrinate: Fandom is not a simple contagion. It requires a reader to take a risk and then adopt or change behavior based on your reinforcement. A process that helps new entrants find their place and get rewarded for behavior that you want them to exhibit will also help them determine if they are in the right place.

Without proper onboarding, the new readers can lose interest fast. While they have already taken the risk of buying your book, they have to adopt the behaviors that lead to being a good community member. How does your system educate and reinforce the desired behaviors around participating in the community?

Re(enter)tain: To build advantage, we need to build an audience and reduce churn. Emphasis then shifts from winning new readers to holding one who has already purchased. We have already spent the money to win this reader, why not work to keep them around and engaged? Existing readers are nine times more likely to repurchase and more likely to advocate products to others. When you treat them like a valued member, they will begin to associate their identity with your group and brand.

THE CONNECTIVE TISSUE - HUMAN GIVENS

You now understand the human givens and their importance. They are the emotional glue that holds the entire system together.

In each phase of the cycle, you need to weave in the human givens. Your use of icons, sacred words, and rituals is vital for blurring the real and story world, and creating pattern matches for triggering behavior.

If we are trying to get fans to help us sell books, you can go to the tired old call to action of *"buy my book,"* or you can associate the purchase of your latest book with an act of belonging or gaining intimacy with your hero.

The closer that patterns in the real world can be to patterns presented in your story world, the more power they will possess.

START

 "You don't have to be great to start, but you have to start to be great."

— ZIG ZIGLAR

Every author starts from zero. This section provides a foundation for you to build cumulative advantage right from the beginning.

There is no way to make this process go faster, and if you don't start on the right foot, it will take longer. Expecting to blast off into the lofty sub-one-hundred ranks on your first book is setting yourself up for disappointment; you create an internal conflict when you have a burning urgency for instant success while trying to build a lifelong career in an industry. Give this process the time it requires.

COMPELLING FICTION

Your skill as a writer is the single biggest driver of your success. I don't say this as an excuse in case what I've provided doesn't work, but to give you the cold, hard truth. The prime reason most authors never earn more than $10,000 in their lifetime is that their stories suck. That being said, I've seen authors become very successful – though I struggle to read a page of their work – simply because the story is perfect for an audience that buys books.

IDENTIFYING YOUR MARKET

This goes hand in hand with writing exciting fiction. If you're not concerned with getting paid for writing, then you don't need to know your audience. You can write just for yourself. However, if you expect strangers to exchange their hard-earned money for your books, then you need to know what they like and make sure your work strikes a chord with that audience.

You also need to understand the size of the niche you plan to serve with your writing. Romance is a big genre with hundreds of subgenres, many able to support authors making six and seven figures. Some genres aren't large; not that they can't support you, just be realistic about the market size and your expectations.

A RELEASE STRATEGY

You may have heard about release strategies that help your books get more traction. Inherent in the virtuous marketing cycle are multiple releases; rather than complicate this starting phase, focus on getting a short story and your first book completed.

Accomplishing this work will put you into an elite class of authors: those who have published a book. If it is like most freshman releases, you'll sell a few hundred copies. Then, in less than thirty days, rank gravity will suck your book into the depths of obscurity.

This is the first step for every author who earns a living from writing – putting out the best book they have in them. You can adjust your launch techniques later, once you have a book published. With a published work under your belt, you now have experienced how long it will take you to produce a work, thus informing the time between your launch cycles.

Most authors waste time and money trying to plan the "perfect" first launch. Perfect is the enemy of good. Conserve your energy and capital to produce a great first book and a short story. Note that this short story can't be a throwaway; it has to represent your work and compel the reader to buy your first book once it's released.

WHAT SHOULD YOU SPEND YOUR MONEY ON?

My prime focus for authors is finding the best use of capital to get you where you want to go. Right now, it is becoming a published author. This means your money needs to go into only two things: making a great product, and finding your fans. At this point in your career, you won't need advertising to find your audience. Everything you need is in this chapter.

PRODUCT PRODUCTION AND QUALITY

The most challenging part of starting is getting the words out and on paper. This doesn't cost you anything but time and a part of your soul. The other things you'll need are exceptional book covers for your short story and first book, and a talented editor. With these in place, you'll be able to get a book to market. Will it be your best book? Hopefully not, but it will be your most important book because it's the first one to get to market.

That being said, assume that when you go back to read your first book years later, you'll cringe. That's a sign of a growing writer. Time seasons you, and experience improves your work.

FINDING YOUR AUDIENCE

We are looking to build your base audience so they can find future audience members. You won't need to do any advertising, and this can be done at a low cost if you have created the short story to give away as a sample. By joining promotions in the genre in which you write, you can get the names of readers.

Later in accumulate and indoctrinate you will consolidate your new subscribers and coach them to read your book, but first focus on getting your readers on an email list.

I hope after getting this far into the book, you don't have a resistance to doing this work. I've met a lot of authors who, when they ask me how to succeed, are more than ready to dive into advertising, but won't do the work to craft an experience for email subscribers. By building a solid bunch of email automations now while you're writing your book, you'll have a way to gather and keep your readers.

EMAIL

Email will be your dominant method of building an audience. You'll need:

> **An email service provider**: like mailchimp, mailerlite or convertkit. While some services offer a free program for limited subscribers, eventually this will become a monthly recurring cost for you.
> **BookFunnel and/or Story Origin:** These two services offer book promotions, and deliver your book to a reader when they sign up. Best of all, they are widely accepted by readers as a provider of books.

Newsletter swaps: I feel author newsletter swaps are by far the best way to build your audience in the beginning rounds. If you can get authors you admire to share your short story link in their newsletter, you'll gain access to a focused audience of prospects. Readers of your genre are so into the content, they sign up for newsletters.

In the beginning, this can seem daunting. You either have no list or a tiny one, so why would they want to swap with you when they have a list and you don't? Simple – they were you once. Many authors are more than happy to pay it forward and give you a feature. This costs nothing, and the more you ask, the more opportunities you'll get.

There are several genre-focused newsletter swap groups on Facebook. Join them, and start signing up with other authors for swaps.

A word of caution: make sure you follow through and share others' books at the agreed time. You are building a peer community as well, and a quick way to ruin your reputation is not to share.

Promotions: Paid and free promotions are genre-focused programs to collect readers email addresses by offering books. Some provide other goodies like gift cards and e-readers, but the best are highly targeted at genres and offer well vetted books as the reward for the email. By participating in these promotions, you can quickly build a list of three hundred to a thousand names.

Community: This may seem absurd when you've not even published your first book, however, if you are looking to create an experience for your readers, you need to put the infrastructure in place for your community to congregate. There is nothing wrong with clarifying that the community is new, and there will be more to come. As you mature in your career, your community will come into its own. Just make sure that readers who are engaged and interested in connecting with your story world and like-minded fans have a place to connect.

In the beginning, this may only be via email, but later, you can host a community on a platform like your website, Facebook, Patreon, or Mighty Networks.

19
LAUNCH

> *"If you believe you can, you probably can. If you believe you won't, you most assuredly won't. Belief is the ignition switch that gets you off the launching pad."*
>
> — *DENIS WAITLEY*

As the name implies, the virtuous marketing cycle is a series of repeated events. Each round, we look to win more readers, integrate them into our fanbase, and then keep them around for participation in future rounds. The launch phase is still the essential part of the cycle. It provides a limited time frame to maximize visibility. Once that window closes, you can continue to promote the title, but the costs will rise and results diminish.

One particular launch cycle will be your breakout. I've observed this in my client data again and again. It is typically somewhere between books five and twelve, when you launch a book that resonates with a broader audience. The combination of finding your voice, having a base of fans, and showing the market that you're committed to the business, results in a step-change more significant than any launch before. This will create a new floor in your popularity and cumulative advantage.

Expecting this to happen sooner or on your first launch is setting unrealistic expectations. If there is a desperate need to make this happen sooner because of the lack of funds to support your publishing, then you're being impractical about the capital necessary to start this business.

PREORDERS

Running a preorder window of two to four weeks before the launch can give you time to optimize your launch cycle. Using this window to ramp up excitement and fine-tune your advertising and marketing for your first twenty-one days can be helpful. The preorder ad optimization puts you in a position to reduce your management during live launch, and simply adjust spend rather than rewriting ad copy and making image changes.

ADVERTISING

I just mentioned using the preorder period to adjust and test advertising; at some point, you'll try advertising to see if it works for you. My recommendation is that you wait until after you have several books published, and your virtuous marketing cycle, community, and brand are all established. Only then should you start to include advertising strategies.

CELEBRATIONS AND CONTESTS

There is a fundamental tone shift in marketing messages when you celebrate a launch with your fans. This becomes a time for you to use community to promote your book in fun ways.

A typical launch contest is to provide group members with social media posts and banners to share and feature on their personal pages. Rewarding random winners with swag and signed books goes a long way. Using a service like ReaderLinks, you can give fans a trackable link that allows you to see the number of clicks to an Amazon sales page. With this tool, you can run contests and track performance.

Using viral marketing software that tracks user sharing then rewards them with points for completing specific tasks is another way to run contests. I've used UpViral's custom function to reward contestants for buying a book. This is a manual process where the contestant has to enter an order number from Amazon into UpViral, but it works well and allows you to track buyers.

Typically, you need to offer themed prizes that line up with your book launch so that participants are excited to play. This doesn't have to be a big screen TV. My observation has been that the further prizes get away from the theme, the more you dilute the audience. We want to attract readers, not contest junkies.

The point of these contests should reward your existing fans, not try to get new readers. I know this sounds crazy, but sweepstakes and contests with prizes appealing to non-readers can attract those just looking to win something. Many sweepstakes groups share these contests, so your list could grow exponentially, but it would be filled with contest-seekers.

A few years ago, I ran a large contest celebrating the one-hundredth anniversary of a business. We had a huge number of sign-ups, because we gave away ten thousand dollars in prizes over one hundred days, but those names were a mixed bag. Some contest entrants were too lazy to redeem the prizes they won. Others, once they learned what they won (homebrewing equipment and ingredients), didn't want it because they weren't homebrew hobbyists.

Keep your prizes associated with your brand. Author Pippa Grant drives her launches with "boxes of crap" (an inside joke for fans) and logo wear associated with the sports teams from her story world. Dakota Krout, a leading name in GameLit, hosted a launch party on Twitch and gave away pizzas to fans that answered trivia questions, creating a virtual gamers pizza party. He has also given away signature eyeglass frames (with your prescription) in 2020. For fans this makes sense because he is a master of puns and he wears similar glasses.

Make this phase fun and inclusive for your fan base. Their wins are your wins. Don't worry, they'll buy your book because they are already a fan. Now you need them to activate other fans and find new ones for you.

Yes, we want to get new readers, and we have a small window to do so. The mindset shift is that by getting existing fans energized for the launch window, however small this group is, their purchases will influence the marketing amplifiers to attract those new fans.

BUDGET

I suggest spending fifty percent of your marketing and advertising budget in launch phases. We do need to commit budget to retention and general awareness, but the launch cycle is when you have something to sell that your audience is interested in buying.

When I suggest fifty percent of your budget, it doesn't mean it all has to go to advertising. While ads can help reach new readers, the more you can focus on existing fans and readers, the better your results will be.

This is counterintuitive and challenges all the current teaching about paid traffic. Yes, traffic is important, but if it isn't the right traffic, then what good is it? However, money spent on existing fans will strengthen your community, which will respond by spreading the news through word of mouth, providing you with user-generated content, and creating written and verbal social proof.

20
ACCUMULATE

> *Another mode of accumulating power arises from lifting a weight and then allowing it to fall.*
>
> — CHARLES BABBAGE

How easy do you make it to become your fan? Most businesses suck at customer accumulation and are even worse at retention. It's not your fault. It's human nature. When it comes to growing a company, we focus on getting the customers we don't have. Ironically, when there is a downturn, what causes us the most pain is the loss of existing customers. It seems we only appreciate how important they are once they leave.

Where do you want fans to gather?

For most, the initial location is email. It is easy to automate and provides information at a low cost in a format that readers enjoy. My observation is that you need to have both an email system and a community. Email serves certain readers, and they will be happy with what it provides as far as interaction. Where you'll improve the process is focusing on ways for them to better connect with your story world via email sequences.

As you read through the next two chapters, "Indoctrinate" and "Re(enter)tain," you'll see recurring themes. This is because we are now building out the systems that find readers where they are on a customer journey. We want to have a system that requires minor effort by the reader to find their place in the fan community.

EMAIL

Implementing a series of automated emails that welcomes and guides the reader to various types of interaction is critical. This is another place where you must be patient and build better and better automations. As you create your engine, it will be essential to begin you them to help the reader understand your brand fantasy. Have an objective as to what you want the reader experience and how you can enrich the experience.

COMMUNITY

As much as you might hate the idea, you need to build a community. This is for your fans, not you, and it becomes the nucleus of cumulative advantage. The virtuous marketing cycle propels the process, acting as the interest rate. Without an account balance to apply that interest rate to, it won't grow. You need the bank account that holds the principal. Community is just that.

Make sure you have some basic systems in place to help get your fans into the community. In the beginning, this may feel like a doctor's waiting room with nothing to do but read old magazines. But as your story world grows more enriched, you can bring more of it into the community.

21
INDOCTRINATE

> *"If you have the opportunity to do amazing things in your life, I strongly encourage you to invite some to join you."*
>
> — SIMON SINEK

A three to five-email sequence isn't an indoctrination. Most authors provide the same chain of emails to "warm up" the reader, so how are you differentiating yourself? Likely not much, if you're following the typical digital marketing cycle of providing some value, then asking for the sale.

Yes, you're in the business of selling books, and you should never forget that, but also don't forget how you like to be treated. How quickly do you see through a sales sequence and expect the call to action?

Indoctrination is a broader, longer process that helps your fans find where they fit best in your community and, when appropriate, sells books.

Let me clarify what I mean.

Having a lead magnet that offers a sample of your writing in exchange for an email address is a powerful tool. I believe that you should use this marketing method regardless of where you are in your career. Once the prospect downloads your reader magnet, the aim should be to get them to buy from you.

The issue is that we often forget the intermediate step of getting the prospect to read the free book.

Again, our assumptions may be our undoing; pushing through a quick sequence to get to the call to buy more books assumes that the prospect even read our first book. I suggest looking at every step of the process, and putting in place prompts to get a reader to get the full experience. Reading the book is a necessary step.

People rarely read the instruction manual. If you put the effort into guiding them, then your results will improve because you make it easier for them to know what to do.

ORGANIC INDOCTRINATION

Treating a reader that has signed up from a book they paid for the same way you'd treat a reader magnet lead is a fatal error. They are already a buyer, and now they are a buyer signaling an affinity to your brand. In this case, your marching orders are to focus on experience and segmentation. This shouldn't be salesy. I wouldn't have any calls to action that are deal-focused. The indoctrination sequence(s) should help the reader navigate your backlist to read more books with the objective of going deeper into the story world and finding their place in your community. In that process, they will buy more books.

SEGMENT

Segmentation is the idea of using reader characteristics to identify groups of like readers to provide them customized content. What if I like your books but only want to know when the next one is out? Do you put me on a select list that only notifies me of new releases? The case may be that, down the road, I may be more interested, but if I'm a voracious reader in a busy genre like romance, I'm subscribed to hundreds of authors.

This type of reader doesn't read your emails. They only skim subject lines for notification of a release. Giving a reader the chance to opt in to notifications and opt out of pictures of your dog is an example of listening to the customer. Understand that the members of that select list may not even open the email; once they see the subject line, they'll delete it and just buy the book, never giving the "opened email" trigger a chance to fire.

The point of segmentation is to give your customers a chance to tell you more about themselves, thus giving you an opportunity to provide the right treatment, and make them feel included and like you're listening.

The readers who want to be more involved will need guidance as to how they might participate. A big part of this isn't you lording over fans, but helping them build the group they want that will attract like-minded individuals.

USING CHARACTER AND STORY WORLD TO SEGMENT

If you steep your onboarding and indoctrination sequence in your story world, then you can use your story world and characters to help you segment by aligning people, places, and things with various human givens. Is there a location in your story world that represents belonging? Use this icon to guide those looking to belong to a particular segment.

Segmentation can also be done through conversations with your characters. I've seen some fantastic examples where authors have used surveys and quizzes to gather personal details, then used advanced email automations to reply in personalized emails.

WORKING YOUR BACK CATALOG

Use a sequence to indoctrinate and guide a reader through your back catalog. You're intimate with the catalog, and no one understands it as you do. If the back catalog includes series that are interconnected with crossing timelines and guest appearances of your characters, assuming readers have an understanding is a costly mistake.

If you're like most authors, your writing gets better over time, even in your flagship series. Allude to this to lure readers to read deeper into your catalog. Use automation and sequences to coach a reader through your backlist. To do this well can be a lot of work, a complex series of automations, lists, and tags. What's the payoff? Imagine increasing your sales or page reads by five percent without writing another book. Better still is, once the automation is in place, it will pull future readers into the sequence and coach them through the books.

This is all about fostering an experience. Fortunately, your customer likes to read, so if your emails and sequence are engaging and experiential, you boost open rates, engagement, and, best of all, give your fans an impressive reading experience.

BEGIN WITH THE END IN MIND

It is a big help in designing any indoctrination sequence or process to think through what information and experience you want the individual to have. When finished, what should they know, and what resources should they have access to?

Keep in mind that sequences should be simple and provide reinforcement. Whenever possible, use characters or other fans to do the indoctrination and support. Finally, align the experience with meeting and fulfilling human givens.

I know much of this chapter has been focused on email; indoctrination also has an important place in your community, but most readers will find their way to your community via email, back matter, or your website. The question is, what do you have for indoctrination processes to help the fan find where they fit and feel comfortable?

Build processes that make you a better host. As soon as possible, get fans interacting with other fans.

22
RE(ENTER)TAIN

 "I would rather entertain and hope that people learned something than educate people and hope they were entertained."

— *WALT DISNEY*

Readthrough and retention work hand in hand. For many authors, the only reason they can advertise profitably is that enough of their acquired consumers read through their backlist to provide a net positive cash-flow. The facts for authors are harsh when promoting such a low-priced item like a ebook for $3.99; just do some rough math to see the issue. If you pay fifty cents a click and sell a book every five clicks, you need to sell the book for at least $3.60 to break even. If it is a Kindle Unlimited book, they need to read 555 pages to break even. Without readthrough, it will be hard to run long-term profitable advertising.

This isn't a call for you to feverously bang out a backlist, but to show you how important it is to keep fans around.

If you have won a new reader, we want to reduce the chances that, between books, that reader flits off to somewhere else and forgets about us. We need to retain this reader by entertaining them, thus the mash-up of Re(enter)tain.

The best place to start is helping them work through your backlist. Using the community and email sequences to help your reader find the path will improve your readthrough. Coach them through your backlist using free bonus material that triggers moving through the sequence. An example is epilogues or bonus material that is only provided in an email sequence. While this will require some thought and the development of multiple email sequences, there is a big payoff. Once the system is in place, you improve your readthrough probability for every new reader. What would your revenues look like if you increased readthrough by ten percent?

If you have a backlist, then you can build a sequence to shepherd your flock through that backlist. If it feels like I'm beating this backlist thing to death is because it is so profitable when done right. If you are just beginning and don't have a list, then what you do with your non-book content (email, newsletter, and community) becomes vital to keeping gained readers. Having other content holds true for authors with a backlist as well, because voracious readers can burn through your catalog quickly, and then what?

This is where community plays a more significant role. Having a fun and safe place to keep exploring the story world with like-minded people keeps those fans close for your next launch.

23

WHAT ABOUT NON-FICTION?

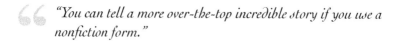 *"You can tell a more over-the-top incredible story if you use a nonfiction form."*

— CHUCK PALAHNIUK

I have focused most of this book on the fiction author. I mainly discuss fiction because I've done most of my research and work with fiction authors. If you are a nonfiction author, don't feel excluded. Much of what I have covered will apply to you.

You might think this method can't help you when I focus on the connection made inside your reader's brain where imagination is formed. It's true that fiction authors have it easier in some ways. The very act of reading fiction requires the reader to use memory, association, and the limbic system to facilitate the process. A nonfiction author also plays in this space, but their work has concepts and ideas that engage other areas of the brain. In these cases, leaning more on the use of the rational and metaphorical mind can help the reader to comprehend complex ideas.

It always goes back to the human givens, meaning that if I don't feel that the book helps me improve my status, belonging, self-actualization, or other critical human givens, I won't see the value.

Take this book as a case in point. Why have you read this far? None of what I discuss here is vital to your basic human survival. The reason is you seek to better yourself through success in your writing business. To actualize this success, you are prepared to learn and develop skills that others wouldn't waste any time on.

More often than not, a nonfiction book is read and never acted upon. This is because while the message is a simple contagion, the behavior change is not. Getting someone to adopt and act on a complex idea is difficult.

Think about this book. All the research and work I've done won't translate to change in an author unless they believe in and adopt the concepts.

Here is where community can be so powerful for a nonfiction author. Using your community to support and reinforce the behaviors needed for your book to succeed will cause the feeling of satisfaction.

If what you are an expert in has an aspirational aspect, then the community can do your heavy lifting. Designing a community whose members support each other and then delivering success will close the loop on your brand promise. For many nonfiction authors, their user group can be a paid membership and become a revenue opportunity as well as a community. It is in this community where you can reinforce behavior to adopt the changes you suggest. A group that is focused on aspiration and achievement of professional or human need becomes the galvanizing rod for your cumulative advantage.

If your end goal is to earn a living from speaking or consulting, cumulative advantage can be used to build your business. Similar to the stockbroker example I provided earlier in the book, as you deliver value for clients, you create resources you can use in future rounds. When you help a client succeed, they become your walking advertisement and you increase the probability of them advocating your book.

Years ago, I went to a motivational seminar. It was held in a stadium because the headliners were Stephen Covey and General Norman Schwarzkopf. Before they went on, there was a string of other speakers.

In the middle of the line-up was Tony Robbins. His presentation was good and stood out from the rest of the crowd, but at that time, he was just a little above a nobody. I'm sure he was doing okay financially, but he was still very far from where he is today in terms of popularity and celebrity status. He was slugging it out, getting his material polished, and building an audience. He was building cumulative advantage.

The resources he accumulated in those rounds where he was the opening act became the resources he could apply and leverage in later rounds. Now he meets with world leaders and celebrities. He charges thousands of dollars for sessions, and we can trace it all back to building an audience focused on meeting the human need to reach your full potential.

AFTERWORD

 "One must have the courage of one's vocation and the courage to make a living from one's vocation."

— PABLO PICASSO

You may feel like your journey has just begun. With the knowledge you now possess, you look at your publishing business and feel like there is more to do than has been done. In your heart, you always know there would not be some quick and easy fix to getting more readers, but now you likely feel more overwhelmed, given what you see as the work you need to do.

This is a common problem for a creative. You are looking over the gap between where you are now and what you can imagine as a perfect cumulative advantage system. This gap only exists in your mind. It's not real.

What is real is that very few authors have done any work toward building a cumulative advantage engine. Those who have weren't all that deliberate about its creation, so their success has more to do with luck than skill. I know this from my interviews with various authors who I feel are building community and brand in a way that creates cumulative advantage.

The conversation goes quickly from them being able to explain to me why something worked, to me explaining to them why it has worked. Their intuition was on the mark, but they didn't know what was making it work so well. Now with a framework, they can see what to do next that will improve the experience and optimize their business.

Publishing is like any other business; it requires continuous process improvement to grow and prosper. This isn't a situation where you just go out and get five pounds of cumulative advantage, and your job is done. As I discussed earlier, there are three parts to your success: natural talent, skill, and luck. You may not be the most talented marketer there is, but by getting through this book, you have increased your skills exponentially. You can continue to improve this particular set of skills, and with their improvement, you will become luckier with your marketing.

Getting even a remedial system in place tips advantage your way. It's the difference in playing Monopoly knowing that everyone has a higher probability of landing in the fifteen spaces after jail than the rest of the board. With that knowledge, you become a tougher opponent. You seem luckier; you're not, you've just made it so that probability is tilted in your favor.

Getting the industry's probabilities to tilt your way is how to build the best cumulative advantage system you can. With each successive round, you will accumulate more resources that you can reinvest in future rounds.

What Is It You Want From Your Writing?

Anyone can write and publish a book on the largest book purveyor in the world. For most authors, that isn't enough. They want to make a living from their creativity. Every one of us who daydreamed in class or spent countless hours reading is compelled to show the skeptics that we can turn that creativity and imagination into cold hard cash.

Achieving the goal of earning a living from your writing will cause two things. One, you'll have a business, and two, you'll have customers.

Your writing becoming a business is a blessing, not a curse. When your success delivers a profit, you'll get more responsibilities. Paying taxes and managing cash flow is the boring part of success, but the alternative is a failing business. Embrace entrepreneurship and making money from your creative endeavors.

If you're any good at this writing thing, you might start impacting people just as you've been affected by a book you read, to the point it changed you, it rewired your thinking and became part of who you were. That author did that by connecting with you at the level of human need, not by swift marketing and aggressive copy with a call to action. You don't recall the marketing, you remember that cover capturing your attention, and the feeling of wanting to experience the book's promise. The authors who deliver on that promise become part of who we are, and if you're an author, that has been the case so much so, it has compelled you to write yourself.

At this point, I suspect you've bought into the idea that cumulative advantage is the force propelling top authors to success. It's not hackable, but it can be built systematically. It all begins with connecting with readers at an emotional level. This is the only *sustainable* solution.

While authors before you may have had it easier because the market was less crowded or advertising was less expensive, they find themselves hostages to the same forces of rank gravity and cumulative advantage. By embracing the ideas I've outlined, authors who thought their career had stagnated, and consigned to a writing treadmill with higher ad costs, have found just the opposite. On fewer books with half the ad spend, they are growing sales, subscribers, and membership.

If you are an established author, then the next step is shifting to building your virtuous marketing cycle. The resources you've accumulated to date will be the account balance that advantage can accumulate upon. If your new to the game, take the viewpoint of a new young tennis player just entering the professional phase. You need time to get experience and establish your standing. In no time, you'll see advantage begin to accumulate, and your audience will grow.

Would you like to continue to do this work? Why not join like-minded authors to share ideas about building your communities, cumulative advantage, and treating your writing like a business? This is a closed group where we explore the ideas of cumulative advantage, reader-focused marketing, and growing a publishing business. All are welcome, and there is no cost. I and the group would love to hear more about how you've applied what you've learned in this book toward building your audience and brand.

Think of this group like owning Tennessee Avenue in Monopoly. Your participation improves your cumulative advantage skill-building. You can connect with fellow authors who seek to build cumulative advantage, and share ideas on what works and what hasn't.

You can always sign up for my Treat Your Writing Like a Business Newsletter to get updates on what I'm working on next.

Joe Solari
    Joe@Joesolari.com

ACKNOWLEDGMENTS

I would like to thank the following people for helping me to put this book together.

First off, my life partner and one true love, Suze Solari. She is always a great cheerleader, sounding board, and helper, recently keeping the house as sane as possible with a move, COVID, and remote learning. Her efforts made it possible for me to get this work done.

I would also like to give a special thanks to Lisa Gardina, who has helped me, and our clients find the best path through uncertain financial times.

I would like to give a special shout out to Jono Bacon, Daryl Weber for talking with me about their work on community and brand. Also a thank you to Alex Newton at K-lytics for his data and acting as a sounding board. A special thanks to Takashi Iba for use of his material in my book.

I owe the following list of authors for opening up the kimono and letting me see how they are doing what they do; thank you Pippa Grant, Chris Kennedy, Martha Carr, Dakota Krout, Nick Cole, Jason Anspach, and Craig Martelle for taking the time to share with me how you have built your businesses.

On the production side, I would like to thank J Thorn, Michelle Scott and Jen McDonnell for the work done to make this a better book.

ABOUT THE AUTHOR

Joe Solari was born and raised in the Chicago Illinois area Joe attended the School of the Art Institute of Chicago where he was conferred a BFA and later earned a MBA from ChicagoBooth School of Business.

He has owned and operated several businesses over his career including working overseas in Australia for four years and a joint venture in India. He has extensive financing experience for small business covering the spectrum of bootstrapping as well as raising over 21 million dollars in less than 18 months for one start-up.

Since 2016 he has worked with authors as private clients.

ALSO BY JOE SOLARI

The definitive guide on how to run a publishing business. Includes the book, community and online course.

Treat Your Writing Like a Business

NOTES

INTRODUCTION

1. Erik Brynjolfsson, Yu Jeffrey Hu, and Michael D. Smith, "The Longer Tail: The Changing Shape of Amazon's Sales Distribution Curve," *SSRN Electronic Journal*, 2010, https://doi.org/10.2139/ssrn.1679991.

1. HOW BIG IS THE PUBLISHING INDUSTRY?

1. Chris Anderson, "The Long Tail," Wired, October 1, 2004, https://www.wired.com/2004/10/tail/.
2. Erik Brynjolfsson, Yu Jeffrey Hu, and Michael D. Smith, "The Longer Tail: The Changing Shape of Amazon's Sales Distribution Curve," SSRN Electronic Journal, 2010, https://doi.org/10.2139/ssrn.1679991.
3. Market report Alex Newton, https://k-lytics.com/
4. Machar Reid et al., "Tournament Structure and Nations' Success in Women's Professional Tennis," *Journal of Sports Sciences* 25, no. 11 (September 1, 2007): 1221–28, https://doi.org/10.1080/02640410600982691.
5. "The Richest Person in the World Every Decade from 1820 to 2020," lovemoney.com, accessed July 23, 2020, https://www.lovemoney.com/galleries/74533/richest-person-every-decade-1820-2020.
6. Michael J. Mauboussin, *The Success Equation: Untangling Skill and Luck in Business, Sports, and Investing* (Harvard Business Review Press, 2012).

3. WINNER TAKES ALL: UNDERSTANDING CUMULATIVE ADVANTAGE

1. This graph was created using data from the September 2019 K-lytics Cozy Mystery Seminar. Revenue estimates are made by the author using estimated daily book sales for each rank, average book price and 365 days of sales. This is a simplified estimate given each title would have its own sales decay and rank change over the year
2. Thomas A. DiPrete and Gregory M. Eirich, "Cumulative Advantage as a Mechanism for Inequality: A Review of Theoretical and Empirical Developments," *Annual Review of Sociology* 32, no. 1 (July 6, 2006): 271–97, https://doi.org/10.1146/annurev.soc.32.061604.123127.
3. Thomas A. DiPrete and Gregory M. Eirich, "Cumulative Advantage as a Mechanism for Inequality: A Review of Theoretical and Empirical Developments," *Annual Review of Sociology* 32, no. 1 (July 6, 2006): 271–97, https://doi.org/10.1146/annurev.soc.32.061604.123127.
4. Robert H Frank and Phillip J Cook, "Winner-Take-All Markets," n.d., 33.

5. Davide Di Fatta, "Small World Theory and the World Wide Web: Linking Small World Properties and Website Centrality," n.d., 15.
6. Reka Albert, Hawoong Jeong, and Albert-Laszlo Barabasi, "The Diameter of the World Wide Web," *Nature* 401, no. 6749 (September 1999): 130–31, https://doi.org/10.1038/43601.
7. Derek Thompson, *Hit Makers: The Science of Popularity in an Age of Distraction*, First Edition edition (New York: Penguin Press, 2017).
8. Derek Thompson, *Hit Makers: The Science of Popularity in an Age of Distraction*, First Edition edition (New York: Penguin Press, 2017).
9. Raymond A. K. Cox, James M. Felton, and Kee H. Chung, "The Concentration of Commercial Success in Popular Music: An Analysis of the Distribution of Gold Records," *Journal of Cultural Economics* 19, no. 4 (1995): 333–40, https://doi.org/10.1007/BF01073995.
10. Takashi Iba et al., "Power-Law Distribution in Japanese Book Sales Market," n.d., 10.
11. Derek Neal, "THEORIES OF THE DISTRIBUTION OF EARNINGS," n.d., 90.
12. Robert H Frank and Phillip J Cook, "Winner-Take-All Markets," n.d., 33.
13. Atul A. Dar and Sal AmirKhalkhali, "On The Growth Process Of Firms: Does Size Matter?," *International Business & Economics Research Journal (IBER)* 14, no. 3 (April 30, 2015): 477, https://doi.org/10.19030/iber.v14i3.9217.
14. Sherwin Rosen, "The Economics of Superstars," *The American Economic Review* 71, no. 5 (1981): 845–58, https://www.jstor.org/stable/1803469.
15. Rosen.
16. Moshe Adler, "Chapter 25 Stardom and Talent," in *Handbook of the Economics of Art and Culture*, vol. 1 (Elsevier, 2006), 895–906, https://doi.org/10.1016/S1574-0676(06)01025-8.
17. M. J. Salganik, "Experimental Study of Inequality and Unpredictability in an Artificial Cultural Market," *Science* 311, no. 5762 (February 10, 2006): 854–56, https://doi.org/10.1126/science.1121066.
18. M. J. Salganik, "Experimental Study of Inequality and Unpredictability in an Artificial Cultural Market," *Science* 311, no. 5762 (February 10, 2006): 854–56, https://doi.org/10.1126/science.1121066.
19. M. J. Salganik, "Experimental Study of Inequality and Unpredictability in an Artificial Cultural Market," *Science* 311, no. 5762 (February 10, 2006): 854–56, https://doi.org/10.1126/science.1121066.
20. Nela Filimon, Jordi López-Sintas, and Carlos Padrós-Reig, "A Test of Rosen's and Adler's Theories of Superstars," *Journal of Cultural Economics* 35, no. 2 (May 2011): 137–61, https://doi.org/10.1007/s10824-010-9135-x.
21. Takashi Iba et al., "Power-Law Distribution in Japanese Book Sales Market," n.d., 10.

4. IS THERE A FORMULA FOR RECOGNITION AND POPULARITY?

1. "The Sveriges Riksbank Prize in Economic Sciences in Memory of Alfred Nobel 2002," NobelPrize.org, accessed July 16, 2020, https://www.nobelprize.org/prizes/economic-sciences/2002/kahneman/facts/.

2. "The Official Licensing Site of Albert Einstein," Albert Einstein, accessed July 16, 2020, http://einstein.biz/
3. "The Official Licensing Site of Albert Einstein," Albert Einstein, accessed July 16, 2020, http://einstein.biz/
4. "Connect with Our Talent," GreenLight Rights, accessed May 21, 2020, https://greenlightrights.com/talent-representation/.

5. SAY MY NAME: HOW TRENDS DEVELOP AND WHY IT'S IMPORTANT TO YOU

1. Damon Centola and Andrea Baronchelli, "The Spontaneous Emergence of Conventions: An Experimental Study of Cultural Evolution," *Proceedings of the National Academy of Sciences* 112, no. 7 (February 17, 2015): 1989–94, https://doi.org/10.1073/pnas.1418838112.
2. Damon Centola and Andrea Baronchelli, "The Spontaneous Emergence of Conventions: An Experimental Study of Cultural Evolution," *Proceedings of the National Academy of Sciences* 112, no. 7 (February 17, 2015): 1989–94, https://doi.org/10.1073/pnas.1418838112.
3. Damon Centola and Andrea Baronchelli, "The Spontaneous Emergence of Conventions: An Experimental Study of Cultural Evolution," *Proceedings of the National Academy of Sciences* 112, no. 7 (February 17, 2015): 1989–94, https://doi.org/10.1073/pnas.1418838112.
4. Damon Centola, Robb Willer, and Michael Macy, "The Emperor's Dilemma: A Computational Model of Self-Enforcing Norms," *American Journal of Sociology* 110, no. 4 (January 2005): 1009–40, https://doi.org/10.1086/427321.

6. YOUR BRAND

1. Daryl Weber, *Brand Seduction: How Neuroscience Can Help Marketers Build Memorable Brands*, 1 edition (Career Press, 2016).
2. Patrick Hanlon, *Primalbranding: Create Belief Systems That Attract Communities*, Reprint edition (Free Press, 2006).

7. YOUR COMMUNITY

1. William von Hippel, *The Social Leap: The New Evolutionary Science of Who We Are, Where We Come From, and What Makes Us Happy* (Harper Wave, 2018).
2. "Instagram Follower Rates 2018 | Mention.Com," accessed May 18, 2020, https://mention.com/en/reports/instagram/followers/.
3. lexiecarbone, "This Is How Much Instagram Influencers Really Cost," Later Blog, April 10, 2019, https://later.com/blog/instagram-influencers-costs/.
4. "Instagram Follower Rates 2018 | Mention.Com," accessed May 18, 2020, https://mention.com/en/reports/instagram/followers/.
5. Jono Bacon and Peter H. Diamandis, *People Powered: How Communities Can Supercharge Your Business, Brand, and Teams* (HarperCollins Leadership, 2019).

6. JEFFREY Travers and STANLEY Milgram, "An Experimental Study of the Small World Problem**The Study Was Carried out While Both Authors Were at Harvard University, and Was Financed by Grants from the Milton Fund and from the Harvard Laboratory of Social Relations. Mr. Joseph Gerver Provided Invaluable Assistance in Summarizing and Criticizing the Mathematical Work Discussed in This Paper.," in *Social Networks*, ed. Samuel Leinhardt (Academic Press, 1977), 179–97, https://doi.org/10.1016/B978-0-12-442450-0.50018-3.
7. JEFFREY Travers and STANLEY Milgram, "An Experimental Study of the Small World Problem**The Study Was Carried out While Both Authors Were at Harvard University, and Was Financed by Grants from the Milton Fund and from the Harvard Laboratory of Social Relations. Mr. Joseph Gerver Provided Invaluable Assistance in Summarizing and Criticizing the Mathematical Work Discussed in This Paper.," in *Social Networks*, ed. Samuel Leinhardt (Academic Press, 1977), 179–97, https://doi.org/10.1016/B978-0-12-442450-0.50018-3.
8. *How Behavior Spreads: The Science of Complex Contagions*, 1 edition (Princeton; Oxford: Princeton University Press, 2018).
9. Mark S. Granovetter, "The Strength of Weak Ties," *American Journal of Sociology* 78, no. 6 (1973): 1360–80, https://www.jstor.org/stable/2776392.
10. Mark S. Granovetter, "The Strength of Weak Ties," *American Journal of Sociology* 78, no. 6 (1973): 1360–80, https://www.jstor.org/stable/2776392.
11. Jacqueline Johnson Brown and Peter H. Reingen, *Social Ties and Word-of-Mouth Referral Behavior*, 1987.
12. Jacqueline Johnson Brown and Peter H. Reingen, *Social Ties and Word-of-Mouth Referral Behavior*, 1987.
13. Fang Wu and Bernardo A. Huberman, "Social Structure and Opinion Formation," *ArXiv:Cond-Mat/0407252*, July 20, 2004, http://arxiv.org/abs/cond-mat/0407252.
14. Fang Wu and Bernardo A. Huberman, "Social Structure and Opinion Formation," *ArXiv:Cond-Mat/0407252*, July 20, 2004, http://arxiv.org/abs/cond-mat/0407252.
15. *How Behavior Spreads: The Science of Complex Contagions*, accessed May 29, 2020, https://www.scribd.com/book/431639280/How-Behavior-Spreads-The-Science-of-Complex-Contagions.
16. *How Behavior Spreads: The Science of Complex Contagions*, accessed May 29, 2020, https://www.scribd.com/book/431639280/How-Behavior-Spreads-The-Science-of-Complex-Contagions.
17. D. Centola, "The Spread of Behavior in an Online Social Network Experiment," *Science* 329, no. 5996 (September 3, 2010): 1194–97, https://doi.org/10.1126/science.1185231.

8. IT'S ALL IN YOUR HEAD

1. Kahneman, *Thinking, Fast and Slow*, 1st edition (New York: FSG Adult, 2013).
2. Benjamin Libet, "Journal of Consciousness Studies," n.d., 11.
3. Benjamin Libet, "Journal of Consciousness Studies," n.d., 11.
4. Chun Siong Soon et al., "Unconscious Determinants of Free Decisions in the Human Brain," *Nature Neuroscience* 11, no. 5 (May 2008): 543–45, https://doi.org/10.1038/nn.2112.

5. Michael S Gazzaniga, "Principles of Human Brain Organization Derived from Split-Brain Studies," *Neuron* 14, no. 2 (February 1995): 217–28, https://doi.org/10.1016/0896-6273(95)90280-5.
6. Michael S. Gazzaniga, *The Consciousness Instinct: Unraveling the Mystery of How the Brain Makes the Mind* (Farrar, Straus and Giroux, 2018).
7. Antoine Bechara and Antonio R. Damasio, "The Somatic Marker Hypothesis: A Neural Theory of Economic Decision," *Games and Economic Behavior* 52, no. 2 (August 2005): 336–72, https://doi.org/10.1016/j.geb.2004.06.010.
8. Paul Ekman and Daniel Cordaro, "What Is Meant by Calling Emotions Basic," *Emotion Review* 3, no. 4 (October 2011): 364–70, https://doi.org/10.1177/1754073911410740.
9. Joe Griffin and Ivan Tyrrell, *Human Givens: The New Approach to Emotional Health and Clear Thinking* (Human Givens Publishing, 2013).
10. Joe Griffin and Ivan Tyrrell, *Human Givens: The New Approach to Emotional Health and Clear Thinking* (Human Givens Publishing, 2013).
11. Joe Griffin and Ivan Tyrrell, *Human Givens: The New Approach to Emotional Health and Clear Thinking* (Human Givens Publishing, 2013).
12. Yusuke Fujiwara, Yoichi Miyawaki, and Yukiyasu Kamitani, "Estimating Image Bases for Visual Image Reconstruction from Human Brain Activity," n.d., 9.
13. Joe Griffin and Ivan Tyrrell, *Human Givens: The New Approach to Emotional Health and Clear Thinking* (Human Givens Publishing, 2013)

9. YOUR SECRET WEAPON

1. David A Oakley and Peter W. Halligan, "Hypnotic Suggestion and Cognitive Neuroscience," *Trends in Cognitive Sciences* 13, no. 6 (June 2009): 264–70, https://doi.org/10.1016/j.tics.2009.03.004.
2. Griffin and Tyrrell, *Human Givens*.
3. Donald Miller, *Building a StoryBrand: Clarify Your Message So Customers Will Listen* (HarperCollins Leadership, 2017).
4. duncan, "The Power of Perseverance - Why I Called Disney 27 Times in 27 Days," *Duncan Wardle* (blog), May 20, 2020, https://duncanwardle.com/the-power-of-perseverance/.
5. Antoine Bechara and Antonio R. Damasio, "The Somatic Marker Hypothesis: A Neural Theory of Economic Decision," *Games and Economic Behavior* 52, no. 2 (August 2005): 336–72, https://doi.org/10.1016/j.geb.2004.06.010.

10. USING THE KEY

1. Bettina Mai, Susanne Sommer, and Wolfgang Hauber, "Motivational States Influence Effort-Based Decision Making in Rats: The Role of Dopamine in the Nucleus Accumbens," *Cognitive, Affective, & Behavioral Neuroscience* 12, no. 1 (March 1, 2012): 74–84, https://doi.org/10.3758/s13415-011-0068-4.
2. Kahneman, *Thinking, Fast and Slow*, 1st edition (New York: FSG Adult, 2013).

14. EMBEDDING CUMULATIVE ADVANTAGE IN YOUR CONTENT

1. Patrick Hanlon, *Primalbranding: Create Belief Systems That Attract Communities*, Reprint edition (Free Press, 2006).
2. Carl Jung, *Modern Man In Search of a Soul*, trans. W. S. Dell and Cary F. Baynes, First Edition (New York: Harcourt Brace, 1955); Joseph Campbell, *The Hero with a Thousand Faces*, Third Edition (Novato, Calif: New World Library, 2008); Joseph Campbell, *The Hero's Journey: Joseph Campbell on His Life and Work*, ed. Phil Cousineau and David Kudler, 2nd Edition (Joseph Campbell Foundation, 2018).
3. Hannah Schmid and Christoph Klimmt, "A Magically Nice Guy: Parasocial Relationships with Harry Potter across Different Cultures," *International Communication Gazette* 73, no. 3 (April 2011): 252–69, https://doi.org/10.1177/1748048510393658.
4. Timothy W Broom, "Presented in Partial Fulfillment of the Requirements for the Degree Master of Arts in the Graduate School of The Ohio State University," n.d., 91.
5. Shanti Ganesh et al., "How the Human Brain Goes Virtual: Distinct Cortical Regions of the Person-Processing Network Are Involved in Self-Identification with Virtual Agents," *Cerebral Cortex* 22, no. 7 (July 2012): 1577–85, https://doi.org/10.1093/cercor/bhr227.

15. HOW TO CREATE A COMMUNITY THAT BECOMES A FEEDBACK LOOP FOR CUMULATIVE ADVANTAGE

1. Jaye L. Derrick, Shira Gabriel, and Kurt Hugenberg, "Social Surrogacy: How Favored Television Programs Provide the Experience of Belonging," *Journal of Experimental Social Psychology* 45, no. 2 (February 2009): 352–62, https://doi.org/10.1016/j.jesp.2008.12.003.
2. https://www.nu.nl/files/IDC-Facebook%20Always%20Connected%20(1).pdf
3. Deborah M. Gordon, *Ant Encounters: Interaction Networks and Colony Behavior* (Princeton University Press, 2010).
4. Ronald S. Burt, *Brokerage and Closure: An Introduction to Social Capital* (Oxford: Oxford University Press, 2007).

17. MAKING IT HAPPEN: BUILDING YOUR CUMULATIVE ADVANTAGE ENGINE

1. Bacon and Diamandis, *People Powered*.

BIBLIOGRAPHY

Albert, Reka, Hawoong Jeong, and Albert-Laszlo Barabasi. "The Diameter of the World Wide Web." *Nature* 401, no. 6749 (September 1999): 130–31. https://doi.org/10.1038/43601.

Anderson, Chris. "The Long Tail." *Wired*, October 1, 2004. https://www.wired.com/2004/10/tail/.

Bacon, Jono, and Peter H. Diamandis. *People Powered: How Communities Can Supercharge Your Business, Brand, and Teams*. HarperCollins Leadership, 2019.

Bechara, A., H. Damasio, D. Tranel, and A. R. Damasio. *Research Focus The Iowa Gambling Task and the Somatic Marker Hypothesis: Some Questions and Answers*, n.d.

Bruyn, Arnaud De, and Gary L Lilien. "A Multi-Stage Model of Word of Mouth Through Electronic Referrals," n.d., 43.

Brynjolfsson, Erik, Yu Jeffrey Hu, and Michael D. Smith. "The Longer Tail: The Changing Shape of Amazon's Sales Distribution Curve." *SSRN Electronic Journal*, 2010. https://doi.org/10.2139/ssrn.1679991.

Burt, Ronald S. *Brokerage and Closure: An Introduction to Social Capital*. Oxford: Oxford University Press, 2007.

Campbell, Joseph. *The Hero with a Thousand Faces*. Third Edition. Novato, Calif: New World Library, 2008.

———. *The Hero's Journey: Joseph Campbell on His Life and Work*. Edited by Phil Cousineau and David Kudler. 2nd Edition. Joseph Campbell Foundation, 2018.

Centola, Damon, and Andrea Baronchelli. "The Spontaneous Emergence of Conventions: An Experimental Study of Cultural Evolution." *Proceedings of the National Academy of Sciences* 112, no. 7 (February 17, 2015): 1989–94. https://doi.org/10.1073/pnas.1418838112.

"Commonlit_asch-Experiment_student.Pdf." Accessed June 12, 2020. https://www.cbsd.org/cms/lib/PA01916442/Centricity/Domain/2773/commonlit_asch-experiment_student.pdf.

GreenLight Rights. "Connect with Our Talent." Accessed May 21, 2020. https://greenlightrights.com/talent-representation/.

"CSM_K-LYTICS_SCIENCE_FICTION_AND_FANTASY_2003_VF.Pdf." Accessed August 15, 2020. https://k-lytics.com/wp-content/uploads/myfiles/custom/CSM_K-LYTICS_SCIENCE_FICTION_AND_FANTASY_2003_VF.pdf.

Dar, Atul A., and Sal AmirKhalkhali. "On The Growth Process Of Firms: Does Size Matter?" *International Business & Economics Research Journal (IBER)* 14, no. 3 (April 30, 2015): 477. https://doi.org/10.19030/iber.v14i3.9217.

Derrick, Jaye L., Shira Gabriel, and Kurt Hugenberg. "Social Surrogacy: How Favored Television Programs Provide the Experience of Belonging." *Journal of Experimental Social Psychology* 45, no. 2 (February 2009): 352–62. https://doi.org/10.1016/j.jesp.2008.12.003.

DiPrete, Thomas A., and Gregory M. Eirich. "Cumulative Advantage as a Mechanism for Inequality: A Review of Theoretical and Empirical Developments." *Annual Review of Sociology* 32, no. 1 (July 6, 2006): 271–97. https://doi.org/10.1146/annurev.soc.32.061604.123127.

duncan. "The Power of Perseverance - Why I Called Disney 27 Times in 27 Days." *Duncan Wardle* (blog), May 20, 2020. https://duncanwardle.com/the-power-of-perseverance/.

Dupre, Kristin B., Corinne Y. Ostock, Karen L. Eskow Jaunarajs, Thomas Button, Lisa M. Savage, William Wolf, and Christopher Bishop. "Local Modulation of Striatal Glutamate Efflux by Serotonin 1A Receptor Stimulation in Dyskinetic, Hemiparkinsonian Rats."

Experimental Neurology 229, no. 2 (June 2011): 288–99. https://doi.org/10.1016/j.expneurol.2011.02.012.

Ekman, Paul, and Daniel Cordaro. "What Is Meant by Calling Emotions Basic." *Emotion Review* 3, no. 4 (October 2011): 364–70. https://doi.org/10.1177/1754073911410740.

Filimon, Nela, Jordi López-Sintas, and Carlos Padrós-Reig. "A Test of Rosen's and Adler's Theories of Superstars." *Journal of Cultural Economics* 35, no. 2 (May 2011): 137–61. https://doi.org/10.1007/s10824-010-9135-x.

Frank, Robert H, and Phillip J Cook. "Winner-Take-All Markets," n.d., 33.

Fujiwara, Yusuke, Yoichi Miyawaki, and Yukiyasu Kamitani. "Estimating Image Bases for Visual Image Reconstruction from Human Brain Activity," n.d., 9.

Gazzaniga, Michael S. "Principles of Human Brain Organization Derived from Split-Brain Studies." *Neuron* 14, no. 2 (February 1995): 217–28. https://doi.org/10.1016/0896-6273(95)90280-5.

Gazzaniga, Michael S. *The Consciousness Instinct: Unraveling the Mystery of How the Brain Makes the Mind*. Farrar, Straus and Giroux, 2018.

Gordon, Deborah M. *Ant Encounters: Interaction Networks and Colony Behavior*. Princeton University Press, 2010.

Granovetter, Mark S. "The Strength of Weak Ties." *American Journal of Sociology* 78, no. 6 (1973): 1360–80. https://www.jstor.org/stable/2776392.

Griffin, Joe, and Ivan Tyrrell. *Human Givens: The New Approach to Emotional Health and Clear Thinking*. Human Givens Publishing, 2013.

Hanlon, Patrick. *Primalbranding: Create Belief Systems That Attract Communities*. Reprint edition. Free Press, 2006.

Hippel, William von. *The Social Leap: The New Evolutionary Science of Who We Are, Where We Come From, and What Makes Us Happy*. Harper Wave, 2018.

How Behavior Spreads: The Science of Complex Contagions. 1 edition. Princeton; Oxford: Princeton University Press, 2018.

How Behavior Spreads: The Science of Complex Contagions. Accessed May 29, 2020. https://www.scribd.com/book/431639280/How-Behavior-Spreads-The-Science-of-Complex-Contagions.

How Behavior Spreads: The Science of Complex Contagions. Accessed May 29, 2020. https://www.scribd.com/book/431639280/How-Behavior-Spreads-The-Science-of-Complex-Contagions.

How Behavior Spreads: The Science of Complex Contagions. Accessed May 29, 2020. https://www.scribd.com/book/431639280/How-Behavior-Spreads-The-Science-of-Complex-Contagions.

How Behavior Spreads: The Science of Complex Contagions. Accessed May 29, 2020. https://www.scribd.com/book/431639280/How-Behavior-Spreads-The-Science-of-Complex-Contagions.

How Behavior Spreads: The Science of Complex Contagions. Accessed May 29, 2020. https://www.scribd.com/book/431639280/How-Behavior-Spreads-The-Science-of-Complex-Contagions.

How Behavior Spreads: The Science of Complex Contagions. Accessed May 29, 2020. https://www.scribd.com/book/431639280/How-Behavior-Spreads-The-Science-of-Complex-Contagions.

Iba, Takashi, Mariko Yoshida, Yoshiaki Fukami, and Masaru Saitoh. "Power-Law Distribution in Japanese Book Sales Market," n.d., 10.

"IDC-Facebook Always Connected (1).Pdf." Accessed June 11, 2020. https://www.nu.nl/files/IDC-Facebook%20Always%20Connected%20(1).pdf.

"Instagram Follower Rates 2018 | Mention.Com." Accessed May 18, 2020. https://mention.com/en/reports/instagram/followers/.

Jung, Carl. *Modern Man In Search of a Soul*. Translated by W. S. Dell and Cary F. Baynes. First Edition. New York: Harcourt Brace, 1955.

Kahneman. *Thinking, Fast and Slow*. 1st edition. New York: FSG Adult, 2013.

Kleinfeld, Judith S. "The Small World Problem." *Society* 39, no. 2 (January 1, 2002): 61–66. https://doi.org/10.1007/BF02717530.

Knoke, David, and Song Yang. *Social Network Analysis*. SAGE Publications, 2019.

lexiecarbone. "This Is How Much Instagram Influencers Really Cost." Later Blog, April 10, 2019. https://later.com/blog/instagram-influencers-costs/.

Libet, Benjamin. "Journal of Consciousness Studies," n.d., 11.

Mai, Bettina, Susanne Sommer, and Wolfgang Hauber. "Motivational States Influence Effort-Based Decision Making in Rats: The Role of

Dopamine in the Nucleus Accumbens." *Cognitive, Affective, & Behavioral Neuroscience* 12, no. 1 (March 1, 2012): 74–84. https://doi.org/10.3758/s13415-011-0068-4.

Mauboussin, Michael J. *The Success Equation: Untangling Skill and Luck in Business, Sports, and Investing.* Harvard Business Review Press, 2012.

Miller, Donald. *Building a StoryBrand: Clarify Your Message So Customers Will Listen.* HarperCollins Leadership, 2017.

Miller, John H., and Scott E. Page. "The Standing Ovation Problem." *Complexity* 9, no. 5 (May 2004): 8–16. https://doi.org/10.1002/cplx.20033.

Reid, Machar, Miguel Crespo, Francisco Atienza, and James Dimmock. "Tournament Structure and Nations' Success in Women's Professional Tennis." *Journal of Sports Sciences* 25, no. 11 (September 1, 2007): 1221–28. https://doi.org/10.1080/02640410600982691.

Salganik, M. J. "Experimental Study of Inequality and Unpredictability in an Artificial Cultural Market." *Science* 311, no. 5762 (February 10, 2006): 854–56. https://doi.org/10.1126/science.1121066.

Scribd. "Schelling Micromotives and Macrobehavior 1978 | Economic Equilibrium | Prices." Accessed May 29, 2020. https://www.scribd.com/document/325140253/Schelling-Micromotives-and-Macrobehavior-1978.

Schmid, Hannah, and Christoph Klimmt. "A Magically Nice Guy: Parasocial Relationships with Harry Potter across Different Cultures." *International Communication Gazette* 73, no. 3 (April 2011): 252–69. https://doi.org/10.1177/1748048510393658.

Albert Einstein. "The Official Licensing Site of Albert Einstein." Accessed May 21, 2020. http://einstein.biz/.

Albert Einstein. "The Official Licensing Site of Albert Einstein." Accessed July 16, 2020. http://einstein.biz/.

lovemoney.com. "The Richest Person in the World Every Decade from 1820 to 2020." Accessed July 23, 2020. https://www.lovemoney.com/galleries/74533/richest-person-every-decade-1820-2020.

NobelPrize.org. "The Sveriges Riksbank Prize in Economic Sciences in Memory of Alfred Nobel 2002." Accessed July 16, 2020. https://www.nobelprize.org/prizes/economic-sciences/2002/kahneman/facts/.

Thompson, Derek. *Hit Makers: The Science of Popularity in an Age of Distraction*. First Edition edition. New York: Penguin Press, 2017.

Travers, JEFFREY, and STANLEY Milgram. "An Experimental Study of the Small World Problem**The Study Was Carried out While Both Authors Were at Harvard University, and Was Financed by Grants from the Milton Fund and from the Harvard Laboratory of Social Relations. Mr. Joseph Gerver Provided Invaluable Assistance in Summarizing and Criticizing the Mathematical Work Discussed in This Paper." In *Social Networks*, edited by Samuel Leinhardt, 179–97. Academic Press, 1977. https://doi.org/10.1016/B978-0-12-442450-0.50018-3.

"Travers1969.Pdf." Accessed July 17, 2020. http://www.uvm.edu/pdodds/teaching/courses/2009-08UVM-300/docs/others/1969/travers1969.pdf.

Watts, Duncan J. *Six Degrees: The Science of a Connected Age*. Reprint edition. New York: W. W. Norton & Company, 2004.

Weber, Daryl. *Brand Seduction: How Neuroscience Can Help Marketers Build Memorable Brands*. 1 edition. Career Press, 2016.

Wu, Fang, and Bernardo A. Huberman. "Social Structure and Opinion Formation." *ArXiv:Cond-Mat/0407252*, July 20, 2004. http://arxiv.org/abs/cond-mat/0407252.

INDEX

A

Advertising:
  Amazon's focus — 130
  deferred — 189
  diminishing returns — 52
  disadvantages — 131
  profitability — 31
  spend. top authors — 37
  transaction-focus — 4
  word of mouth — 88–89
algorithms — 19, 20, 139
Analogies:
  climbing — 32–33
  forest fire — 93–94
  Harvester ants — 155–56
  investing — 44–45
  Monopoly — 37–38
  tennis — 21–23
Anderson, Chris [author] — 18
anthologies, effect on sales — 32
associations, positive — 112

B

backlist/back catalog — 196–97, 198
Bacon, Jono [author, SCARF system] — 84
Behavior:
  change — 91
  rationalization of choice — 103

Behavior cont/d:
  reinforcing — 154
  risk — 99
beta readers — 168
binge economy — 26–32
book launches — 188–91
book series, effect on sales — 27–30
BookFunnel — 186
brain patterns — 102
Brand:
  anchor — 75–76
  bible — 179
  defining tribe — 79–80
  establishing — 59–60
  fantasy — 78–79, 178–79
  platform — 83
  promise — 76–78, 178
  story — 113
  unifying message — 162
breakouts — 32–33, 188
budget, marketing — 191
Building a Story Brand [book] — 113

C

cash flow stress — 133
character archetypes — 146–49
characters, in brain imaging — 148
climbing analogy — 32–33

Community:
    building   154–57, 193
    connection with characters   153
    Disney   83–84
    human givens   157–58
    opinion   89
    purpose   82
    validation   108
    weak ties   89
competition, corporate   130–31
compounding effect   44, 52, 139
confirmation bias   102
Connection, Emotional:
    effect on cumulative advantage   141
    Einstein   56
    inclusion   110
    names   68
    Somatic Marker hypothesis   78
    with readers   60
Contagions:
    complex   91, 141, 150, 152
    simple   90, 91
contests   189–90
conventions, social
    See Social Conventions
cowriting, effect on sales   32
cultural movements   68
Cumulative Advantage:
    definition   12–14
    embedding via character
        archetypes   146–49
    embedding via lore & canon   149–50
    embedding via story tropes   144–46
    improvement   23
    understanding   34–53
Customer-Focus
    importance of   131, 135
    nurturing   84

D

Damasio, Antonio [neuroscientist]   104
dopamine   119, 143

E

Einstein, Albert   55–60
email marketing   186–87, 192–93
Emotions:
    fulfillment of a human given   121
    negative   153, 163
    pattern-matching   144
    positive   112
    reactions   104

Emotions cont/d:
    social situation   81
    triggered by story   178
    universally recognized   105

F

fandom, similarities   148
fluency   122–26
forest fire analogy   93–94

G

gatekeepers   25
Gazzaniga, Dr Michael   103–4
Gibrat's Law   46–47
Grant, Pippa [author]   190
Greenlight [branding company] 57–59, 72
Groups:
    behavior   165–66, 170
    engagement   172–76
    identity   170
    onboarding   171–72
    roles   166–68
    sub-networks   168–69
    traits, successful   163–64

H

Harvester ants analogy   155–56
Hero's Journey   113, 146, 218
Human Givens Approach   106–7, 109
hypnotic effect   111–12, 113

I

Iba, Takashi Dr   50–51
Ikea effect   173
indoctrination sequence   195
inertia   86–89
influence, social   49–50
inner circle, fans   169
intelligence, collective   71
investing analogy   44–45

J

J curve   35
Jerusalem, Hebrew University of   57, 59

K

Kahneman, Daniel [psychologist & economist]	56–57, 99
Kindle Unlimited	27, 29, 198
Krout, Dakota [author]	190

L

language, special	145–46
launch season	25
launches	188–91
List Building:	
backlist/back catalog	196
indoctrination	194–95
lead magnet	194
segmenting	195, 196
Long Tail, The [article]	18–19, 218
Lotka distribution	39, 41
luck	22, 38, 48

M

market, identifying	184
marketing budget	191
Marketing Cycles:	
vicious	136–38
virtuous	138–40, 181–82
Memory:	
associations	57, 119, 148
disconnect	105
emotional tie	115
fluency	124
readers	171
stories	113
meso-neuro feedback loop	94–95
Milgram, Stanley [psychologist]	85–88
Miller, Donald [author]	113
Monopoly analogy	37–38

N

neurochemical release	119
newsletter swaps	186–87
non-fiction books	200–202

O

organic readers	32

P

Pareto Principle	35, 38–39
Pattern-Matching:	
brain expectation	98
brand	77
characters	145
human givens approach	109
reading	119–26
recognition	60
sensory input	102
ways to implement	121–22
People Powered [book]	84
personality profiling	148
plateau, rank	*See* rank plateau
plateaus	29, 32–33
Power Laws:	
Internet, sports & music	39–42
publishing	42–43
preorders	27, 161–62, 189
procrastination	119
psychology, behavioral	78, 139, 181
publishing industry scale	17–19

Q

quality, in relation to social influence	49

R

Rank:	
gravity	24–25, 132, 181
plateau	21, 27, 29, 32–33
reader magnets	*See* List Building
ReaderLinks [author service]	189
Readers:	
limbo	137
organic	32
readthrough	29, 193, 198
Recognition:	
Einstein	59
esteem	157
Kahneman	60
Maslow	106
regret avoidance	46
release strategy	184
results tracking	31
Retention:	
budget	191
engagement	172
focus	137
gym example	167
onboarding	166, 171
readthrough	198
support behaviors	174
revenue peaks	27

Reviews:
    as social proof — 77
    street team — 168
rivalry — 163, 164
Robbins, Tony — 201
Rosen, Sherwin [economist] — 47–48
Rowling, JK — 53

S

sales decay curve — 26–32
Sapkowski, Andrzej [fantasy author] — 53, 162
SCARF model — 84–85, 107
scope & scale, of publishing industry — 17–19
segmentation — 195–96
Shakespeare, William — 120
skill — 22, 183
Social Conventions:
    common — 63
    experiments — 69
    spontaneous — 70
    user agreement — 146
social influence — 49–50
Social Media:
    as placebo — 154
    dopamine — 119
    downsides — 83
social network, designing — 158–61
social proof — 46, 168, 191
socialization — 108
Somatic Marker hypothesis — 78, 104, 116
Story Origin — 186
street teams — 168
success — 31

T

talent — 22, 48

tennis, analogy — 21–23
Thinking, Fast and Slow [book] — 57, 99
tracking results — 31
Trends:
    names — 61–66
    popular culture — 67
    viral — 69
tribe, defining — 176
trigger words — 122

U

UpViral [marketing software] — 190

V

Virality:
    classic — 69
    groundwork — 2
    hope — 85
    inertia — 86
    marketing software — *See* UpViral
    opinion change — 90
    suitability — 88

W

Wardle, Duncan [innovation consultant] — 115
Weber, Daryl [author/brand consultant] — 78
winner-take-all — 36, 49
winner-take-most-results — 12, 40–41
winner-takes-all — 34–53

Z

Zipf Curve/Law — 35, 39

CPSIA information can be obtained
at www.ICGtesting.com
Printed in the USA
LVHW080845220821
695735LV00013B/1186